I0559735

1

The Parallel Histories of Israel and Palestine

Everything you wanted to know but were afraid to ask

Michael Davies

Michael Davies was born in Windsor to a Welsh Baptist father and an Irish Catholic mother and brought up in Northern Ireland and London. He was educated at Dulwich College and Christ Church Oxford where he read Modern History. He lived in New York and Chicago before settling in northwest England to teach history for eighteen years. In 2017 he set up Parallel Histories, an educational foundation to help teachers teach the contested and divisive history of Israel and Palestine. The Parallel Histories method is now used in over 65 countries.

Publisher's note: Michael died in July 2024. He had finished writing this book before his death. His friends have overseen the process to publish the book.

Michael is survived by his wife and four children.

Contents

To Carys

Introduction

This is a book for readers with little or patchy background knowledge of this topic. Its main purpose is to tell the history of Israel and Palestine in the terms that Israelis and Palestinians themselves would tell it. It will also be of interest to readers who do know about Israel and Palestine and have already come down firmly on one side or another. For them, it may be intellectually refreshing to read a historical interpretation which is at odds with their current understanding.

This is a primer. It summarises the history of both Jews and Arabs living in the area between the Mediterranean Sea and the River Jordan in a little over ten thousand words. Most histories of this area – written by Israeli or Palestinian historians (or their respective sympathisers) – address the questions: what are the causes of conflict between Jews and Arabs, Israelis and Palestinians, and which group has the stronger claim to the land? These are also the two questions that underlie most journalistic reporting as well as debate in the media. This book, therefore, addresses the same two questions.

This book is not in any way a detailed history. If you want to know more about a particular event like the Six Day War/Naksa, then there are many better books. Nor does this book contain any of our own original historical research. I have read widely and drawn from the work of hundreds of others. Nor is it a social or cultural history – our focus is on the causes of conflict.

The approach I've adopted is a dual narrative structure – on the left-hand page is the Israeli narrative and facing it on the right-hand page is the Palestinian narrative. We have adopted this structure for two reasons. In the first place it's because no one can agree on a single shared narrative. Ordinary Israelis and Palestinians cannot agree on their shared history, nor can Israeli and Palestinian historians. And that disagreement runs through the history faculties of most universities around the world. The nature of the disagreement can be very large; for example, there's a professional Israeli historian who argues that the massacre of Palestinian villagers at Deir Yassin in 1948 never took place. And there's a professional Palestinian historian who argues that the Deir Yassin massacre establishes that Israel had a master plan to drive Palestinians off the land. Even place names are disputed and one choice or another signifies where the author's sympathies lie. For example, a pro-Israeli historian might refer to

the West Bank as Judea and Samaria, or the Disputed Territories, whereas a pro-Palestinian historian would call it the OPT or Occupied Palestinian Territories. In the second place, there's no better way of understanding the depth of the conflict and its intractability than learning how the history of the conflict is understood by its participants. As a former history teacher, I taught a middle ground watered-down history of the conflict and it left my students puzzled as to why both sides couldn't quickly come to a sensible peace agreement involving a few hard choices on each side; land swaps here, some minor population transfers there, a port and an airport and East Jerusalem as an international city…done and dusted!

Critics of a dual narrative structure are quite right to point out that neither the Israelis nor Palestinians are homogeneous groups. A former Israeli president referred to the "four tribes" of modern Israel: secular, ultra-orthodox, national-religious, and Arab. Palestinians can be categorised by where they live: West Bank, East Jerusalem, Gaza, inside Israel, as semi-nomadic Bedouins or in exile. However, this complexity can be captured as a conflict between two sides, Jews/Israelis, and Arabs/Palestinians. Two narratives enable those who are new to the conflict to understand how and why Israelis and Palestinians narrate the history of the conflict, before going on to explore the varieties of narratives and identities. To avoid anachronism, where possible, we use the term Israeli to describe Jews living in the new state of Israel after 1948 and Palestinian to describe Arabs living in Palestine.

I should also briefly explain how I have organised the material in chapters. You can see from the contents that the approach is broadly chronological. There is one major exception and a couple of minor diversions from that chronological structure. The major exception is that I have used the first chapter to provide a complete historical overview of thousands of years – even in a short book there is value in a summary. The minor diversions are to allow us to deal with a couple of themes over time. It certainly made more sense to treat the 'Peace Process' as one chapter, even though it stretches out across several decades. This is because the obstacles to peace and causes of the failure of the 'Process', as explained by both sides, are almost the same now as they were twenty-five years ago. I

have also treated the chapter on Hamas and Fatah thematically. I have met hundreds of people over the years who admit that while they have a basic grounding in Israeli and Palestinian history, they are almost completely ignorant about Fatah and Hamas, so this is for them.

For most of the book the comparison between an Arab and Jewish historical perspective works very well as an organising principle because there's a very clear difference between the two. However, this is less true for chapters two and three, which cover the period from the Balfour Declaration in 1917 to the end of the British Mandate in 1948. Here I pose two questions: should the British Government be praised or blamed for the Balfour Declaration, and should the British government be praised or blamed for its management of the Mandate? While Palestinians were, and remain, highly critical of the Balfour Declaration and the Mandate, Israeli historical opinion is mixed. Therefore, I've presented these chapters as two sides of an historical argument rather than Jewish versus Arab historical narratives. Britain's role in creating this conflict in the Middle East was pivotal but has almost been forgotten.

Finally, I should explain why it's worthwhile bringing out a book like this. We (everyone involved in the Parallel Histories project) are convinced that it's much healthier for us all if controversial subjects are discussed openly. It helps no one if disagreements are swept under the carpet to avoid causing offence. As societies we have to learn how to disagree without falling out. This little history primer is designed to show that not only is it possible for two opposing ideas to live side by side in a book, but also that the reader will benefit from engaging with both. To quote F. Scott Fitzgerald "The test of a first-rate intelligence is the ability to hold two opposing ideas in mind at the same time and still retain the ability to function." It's a test we all need to try to pass!

CHAPTER 1

A Complete History of Israel and Palestine

Arabs or Jews, which group has the stronger claim to the land?

The Jewish people originated in Eretz, Israel three thousand years ago and until the fourth century AD remained the majority there. From the first to the twentieth century only a few thousand Jews lived in Israel, most were scattered across the globe in tiny minorities, vulnerable to periodic bouts of persecution usually at the hands of Christians. By the 19th century, 60% of Jews in the world lived in an area of Russia called the Pale, and it was here that a particularly long and brutal period of persecution started in the 1880s.

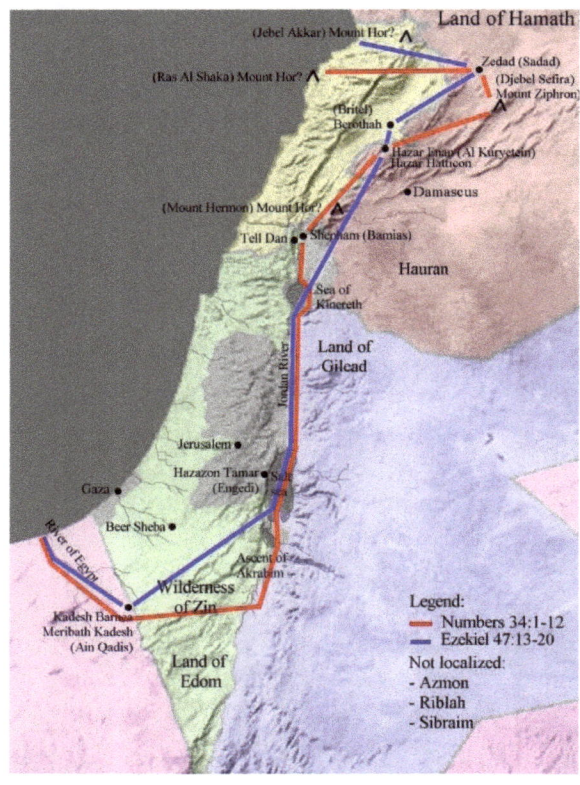

Map of Israel according to the biblical Book of Numbers

Year	Jews	Christians	Muslims
1st.c.	**Majority**	—	—
4th c.	**Majority**	Minority	—
5th c.	Minority	**Majority**	—
6th c.	Minority	**Majority**	—
7th c.	Minority	**Majority**	Minority
8th c.	Minority	**Majority**	Minority
9th c.	Minority	**Majority**	Minority
10th c.	Minority	**Majority**	Minority
11th c.	Minority	**Majority**	Minority
End 12th c.	Minority	Minority	**Majority**
14th c.	Minority	Minority	**Majority**

Population data for Israel/Palestine dating back to the ancient period. Estimates by Sergio Della Pergola, 'Demography in Israel/Palestine: Trends, Prospects, Policy Implications' for the IUSSP XXIV General Population Conference Salvador de Bahia, August 2001

In the middle of the 7th century, tribespeople from the Arabian Peninsula settled much of the modern Middle East, mixed with the local population, and permanently settled the land between the River Jordan and the Mediterranean which they called Jund Filastin. European attempts over two centuries of Crusades to conquer the Holy Land ended in failure in 1291. Three centuries later, the Ottoman Empire expanded to rule the area until 1917. However, the Empire picked the losing side in World War I and was pushed out by a combination of the British army and the Arab Revolt.

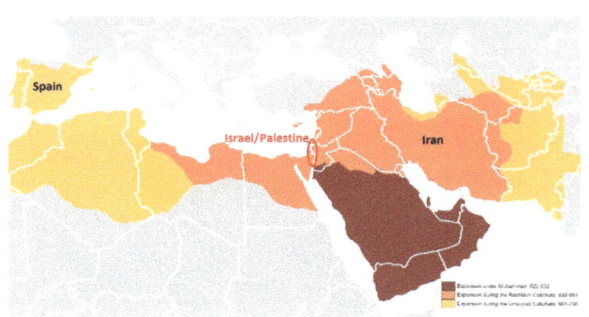

Map of expansion of the Islamic Caliphate, with Israel/Palestine highlighted

Year	Jews	Christians	Muslims
1st.c.	**Majority**	—	—
4th c.	**Majority**	Minority	—
5th c.	Minority	**Majority**	—
6th c.	Minority	**Majority**	—
7th c.	Minority	**Majority**	Minority
8th c.	Minority	**Majority**	Minority
9th c.	Minority	**Majority**	Minority
10th c.	Minority	**Majority**	Minority
11th c.	Minority	**Majority**	Minority
End 12th c.	Minority	Minority	**Majority**
14th c.	Minority	Minority	**Majority**

Population data for Israel/Palestine dating back to the ancient period. Estimates by Sergio Della Pergola, 'Demography in Israel/Palestine: Trends, Prospects, Policy Implications' for the IUSSP XXIV General Population Conference Salvador de Bahia, August 2001

13

This persecution led European Jews to establish the World Zionist Congress in 1897. Their goal was the re-establishment of a Jewish home in the land of Israel, a land promised to the Jews by God in the Hebrew Bible. In 1917 the British government was persuaded by Chaim Weizmann to issue the Balfour Declaration which promised to help Jews create a national home in Palestine. Jews were allowed to immigrate and form a self-governing community. The Jews returning to Israel joined a small community that had never left. As their numbers increased so did friction with local Arabs, with whom they competed for farmland. In the 1930s the British chose to limit Jewish immigration to prevent Arab unrest.

Foreign Office,
November 2nd, 1917.

Dear Lord Rothschild,

I have much pleasure in conveying to you, on behalf of His Majesty's Government, the following declaration of sympathy with Jewish Zionist aspirations which has been submitted to, and approved by, the Cabinet

"His Majesty's Government view with favour the establishment in Palestine of a national home for the Jewish people, and will use their best endeavours to facilitate the achievement of this object, it being clearly understood that nothing shall be done which may prejudice the civil and religious rights of existing non-Jewish communities in Palestine, or the rights and political status enjoyed by Jews in any other country"

I should be grateful if you would bring this declaration to the knowledge of the Zionist Federation.

The Balfour Declaration, 1917

A photograph of the First Zionist Congress in Basel in 1897

14

At this point, Palestinians believed British promises that they would have their own state, or at least be able to govern themselves as part of a larger Arab nation. However, Britain reneged on its deal with the Arabs. It secretly carved up much of the Arab lands with France in the Sykes-Picot agreement. Then the British government continued their betrayal of the Arabs by issuing the Balfour Declaration, a commitment to help Jews build their national home in Palestine. So, Britain not only betrayed their promise of an Arab state, but also helped the Jews to establish a Jewish state on Arab land in Palestine. This is where the conflict between Arabs and Jews began.

Date	Occasion	Substance
14 July 1915 – 30 June 1916	McMahon-Hussein correspondence Sir Henry McMahon was British High Commissioner in England. Sharif Hussein was the ruler of the Emirate of Mecca	The British Government promised support for an independent Arab state in areas then under the rule of the Ottoman Empire in return for an Arab rebellion against the Ottomans.
2 November 1917	Balfour Declaration A letter from British Foreign Secretary, Arthur, to Walter Rothschild, 2nd Baron Rothschild, leader of the British Jewish community.	A promise to the Jews that the British Government would support the establishment of a national home for the Jewish people in Palestine. The letter included the provision that 'nothing shall be done which may prejudice the civil and religious rights of existing non-Jewish communities in Palestine'.
January 1918	Message from the British Government to Sharif Hussein, sent via Commander David George Hogarth	Hogarth's message stated that the 'political and economic freedom' of the Palestinian population was not in question.
16 June 1918	The Declaration to the Seven A British officer read out the declaration to a meeting of seven Arab leaders	The British Government promised independence by the Arabs under the principle of 'consent of the governed'.
7 November 1918	Anglo-French Declaration Copies were posted in Arab towns and villages then occupied by Allied forces, including Palestine	'The object aimed at by France and Great Britain in prosecuting...the War...is complete and definite emancipation of the peoples so long oppressed by the Turks and the establishment of national governments and administrations deriving their authority from the initiative and free choice of the indigenous populations'.

Promises and assurances made to the Arabs 1916-19

Arab Fighters in Akaba Arabia (now Jordan), February 1918. In return for revolting against the Ottomans, the British assured them they would have their own state

15

The shock of the Holocaust clearly demonstrated both to Jews and the rest of the world that a national home was more necessary than ever. Palestinian leader Amin Al-Husseini's meeting with Hitler to request support for Arab independence did not help the Arab cause. There were so many hundreds of thousands of Jewish refugees in Europe that no one country could accommodate them all. Jews did emigrate to the USA and other European countries, but emigration to Palestine also had to be part of the solution. Then, in 1947, the United Nations voted to partition British Palestine into a Jewish and an Arab state. The Jews accepted this but the Arabs rejected it.

A GREAT
PUBLIC DEMONSTRATION
Under the auspices of
THE BRITISH BROTHERS' LEAGUE,
in favour of restricting the further immigration o
DESTITUTE FOREIGNERS
into this Country, will be held at
THE PEOPLE'S PALACE,
MILE END, E., on
TUESDAY, JAN. 14TH, 1902.

The Chair will be taken at Eight p.m. sharp, by
MAJOR EVANS-GORDON, M.P.,
who will be supported by Members of Parliament, County and Borough Councillors, Members of Boards of Guardians of all shades of politics, and Ministers of Religion of all Denominations.

A poster advertising a public meeting in London protesting Jewish immigration caused by pogroms in Russia

A photograph showing Storm Troopers (SA) blocking the entrance to a Jewish-owned shop. One of the signs says: "Germans! Defend yourselves! Don't buy from Jews!" Berlin, Germany, April 1933

Hundreds of thousands of Jews were fleeing persecution in Eastern Europe but neither the USA nor Western European countries were willing to open their doors to these refugees – it was easier to funnel them to Palestine. The same thing happened at the end of the Second World War. The Jews had suffered again at the hands of Europeans Christians, millions were killed and millions were stateless refugees. And again, the Europeans and the Americans closed their doors, and pushed Jews, many of whom wanted to go to the USA, towards Palestine.

"Nor could they [those who drafted the British Mandate in Palestine] have foreseen the complete change in the situation which would be brought about by the drastic restriction of immigration into the United States, the advent of the National Socialist Government in Germany in 1933 and the increasing economic pressure on the Jews in Poland."

The Peel Commission, a British commission to investigate the causes of conflict in Mandatory Palestine, in 1936 noted how unexpected changes were driving Jewish immigration to Mandatory Palestine

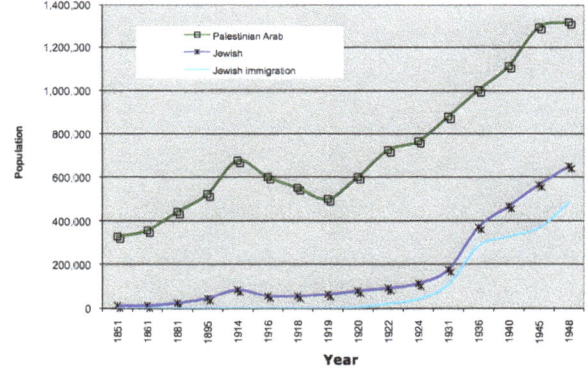

Graph of Jewish immigration to Palestine versus Palestinian Arab population

The armies of the surrounding Arab states attacked Israel immediately after its declaration of independence in May 1948. The new state, led by David Ben Gurion, won this war, and in the process many Palestinian Arabs fled or were forced to leave their villages. There were further wars in 1955, 1967, 1973 and 1982 and there was a major Palestinian uprising known as the First Intifada in 1987. While Israel was always strong enough to protect itself, the continuing problem of Palestinian refugees undermined its relations with both the wider Arab world and the Palestinians.

Photograph showing damage to civilian apartments in Tel Aviv caused by an Egyptian air strike on 16th May 1948

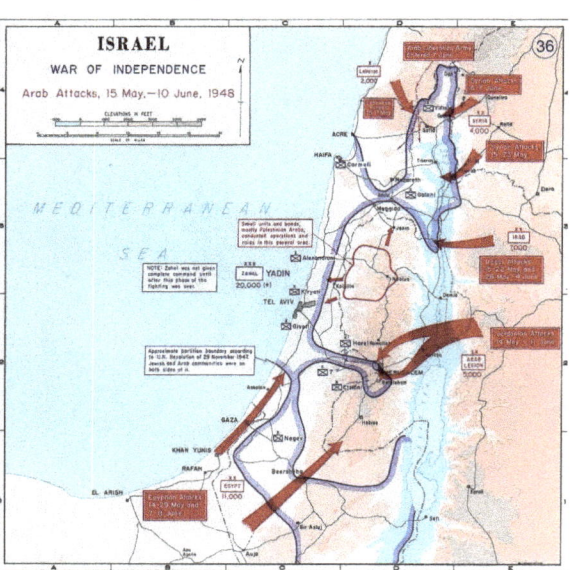

A map made by the US Department of History to teach US Army cadets about the art of war

The United Nations voted to give over half of Palestine to Jews in 1947. War broke between the Jews and the Palestinians, who were supported by the armies of the other Arab nations. Israel defeated the Arab armies and systematically expelled over half the Palestinian population from their homes. Palestinians living in refugee camps never gave up hope and new movements for the liberation of Palestine emerged. Neighbouring Arab nations promised help but as the wars of 1967, 1974 and 1982 showed, they were no match for Israel which used these wars as an opportunity to conquer the rest of Palestine including the West Bank and the Gaza Strip.

Palestinians leaving Galilee during the Nakba, October - November 1948

Extract of Plan Dalet, a military operation carried out by Haganah during the 1948 war. It instructed on the clearing and dismantling of Arab communities.

'Mounting operations against enemy population centers located inside or near our defensive system in order to prevent them from being used as bases by an active armed force. These operations can be divided into the following categories:

Destruction of villages (setting fire to, blowing up, and planting mines in the debris), especially those population centers which are difficult to control cont nuously

Mounting search and control operations according to the following guidelines:
encirclement of the village and conducting a search inside it. In the event of resistance, the armed force must be destroyed and the population must be expelled outs de the borders of the state.'

Extract of Plan Dalet, a military operation carried out by Haganah during the 1948 war. It instructed on the clearing and dismantling of Arab communities

19

Eventually peace treaties were signed with Egypt in 1978 – whereby Israel returned the Sinai – and with Jordan in 1994. Then, the Oslo Accords – signed in the mid 1990s – gave the Palestinians some self-government in return for Israeli security. However, the Oslo Accords were never fully implemented. This was partly because the dysfunctional nature of Palestinian leadership meant that Israel never had a single, clear negotiating partner to work with. In addition, the ruling party in Gaza was an extreme Islamic group called Hamas, sworn to the destruction of Israel. No Israeli government could be expected to negotiate with a terror group dedicated to its destruction.

The Israel-Egypt Peace Treaty. Egyptian President Sadat, US President Carter and Israeli Prime Minister Begin in 1978

On the Destruction of Israel:
'Israel will exist and will continue to exist until Islam will obliterate it, just as it obliterated others before it.' (Preamble)

The Exclusive Muslim Nature of the Area:
'The land of Palestine is an Islamic Waqf consecrated for future Moslem generations until Judgement Day. It, or any part of it, should not be squandered: it, or any part of it, should not be given up.' (Article 11)

'Liberation of Palestine is then an individual duty for every Moslem.' (Article 14)

The Covenant of Hamas, 1988

By the 1980s, unemployment, especially among young Palestinians, was increasing, and food prices were rising. Having lived under Israeli military occupation for 20 years, ordinary Palestinians had no way to express themselves politically. So, in 1987 they rose up against the military occupation in the First Intifada. The Palestinians' peaceful street protests were met with violence by Israeli security forces and Palestinians were forced to defend themselves. World opinion turned against Israel because of TV coverage of unarmed demonstrators being beaten and shot. The USA forced Israel to the negotiating table. The result was the Oslo Accords, which for the first time granted the Palestinians limited self-government.

Israeli soldiers try to order residents of Jabalia in the Gaza Strip to remove a slogan on a wall during the First Intifada

Israeli Prime Minister Rabin, US President Clinton and Palestinian leader Arafat, signing the Oslo Accords in 1993

During the Second Intifada of 2000-2005, many Israeli civilians were killed by Palestinian suicide bombers and this led to the erection of a permanent security fence to protect Israelis. The peace process with Palestinians remains stalled. As Israel has become economically and militarily stronger and more stable, its efforts to improve its relations with its Arab neighbours: Egypt, Iraq, Syria and Lebanon, were frustrated by their internal instability. The majority of Israelis continued to want peace with Palestinians and other Arab states, but not at the expense of their security.

Monument to the victims of a 2002 terror attack committed by a Palestinian suicide bomber near Afula, Israel

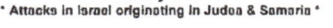
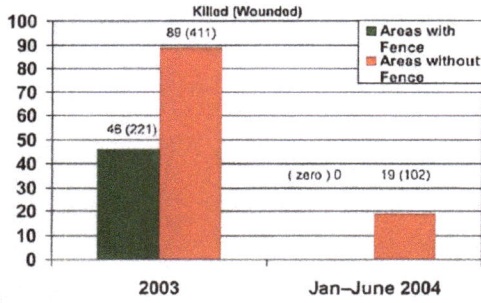

Victims of suicide attacks before & after Security Fence
* Attacks in Israel originating in Judea & Samaria *

Graph published by the Jewish Virtual Library

Israel however never had any intention of giving up the West Bank or Gaza, let alone allowing refugees to return. Defying international law, Israel accelerated the building of Jewish settlements across the West Bank and the Gaza Strip. Israel's policy of pushing the Arab population into urban concentrations, and the building of a separation barrier in 2003, isolated and divided Palestinians. It further strengthened Israel's occupation of the ancient land of Palestine. The cycle of repression, resistance and further repression continues.

Cartoon by artist Naji al-Ali. The child 'Handala' has come to represent Palestinian people for decades. His name is linked to bitter plants originating in Palestine, and he is always depicted as 10 years old, the age Naji al-Ali was forced from his home

PALESTINIAN LOSS OF LAND 1946-2010

A Palestinian map made to show a continuing loss of land, 1946 - 2010

CHAPTER 2

The Balfour Declaration

Should the British Government be praised or blamed for the Balfour Declaration?

November 2nd, 1917.

Dear Lord Rothschild,

I have much pleasure in conveying to you, on behalf of His Majesty's Government, the following declaration of sympathy with Jewish Zionist aspirations which has been submitted to, and approved by, the Cabinet

'His Majesty's Government view with favour the establishment in Palestine of a national home for the Jewish people, and will use their best endeavours to facilitate the achievement of this object, it being clearly understood that nothing shall be done which may prejudice the civil and religious rights of existing non-Jewish communities in Palestine, or the rights and political status enjoyed by Jews in any other country"

I should be grateful if you would bring this declaration to the knowledge of the Zionist Federation.

Jews at the time were not fully satisfied with the content of the Declaration and were sometimes cynical about the British government's motives, but in general they are favourable towards it and Balfour. What looks today like imperial arrogance would have been judged very differently a century ago. The British Empire was fighting three other empires: the German, the Austrian-Hungarian and the Ottoman, and it was natural and prudent that it should plan ahead for the eventuality of the collapse of the Ottoman which was the weakest of the three. The British felt a sense of responsibility for filling the void left by the Ottomans at the end of the war. They did not seize Palestine as they could have done. Instead, the British Government was quick to seek a legal basis from the League of Nations for their Mandate in Palestine.

'I know that the days of this [Ottoman] state are numbered. There is no doubt that it is heading for dissolution sooner or later. But what will be the fate of Palestine after the war? The question is easy to answer. Either independence or our annexation to Egypt.'

Extract from the diary of Ihsan Hasan Turjman, a Palestinian conscript to the Ottoman army. 28 March 1915

ZIONIST REJOICINGS.

BRITISH MANDATE FOR PALESTINE WELCOMED.

News of the conferment of the mandate for Palestine on Great Britain has created a great impression on Zionist and Jewish circles. A prominent Zionist has given the following views to a representative of the London Jewish Correspondence Bureau :—

The news that Great Britain is to have the mandate for Palestine, and the decision to incorporate the Balfour Declaration in the Treaty of Peace with Turkey will be received with intense gratification by Jews in all countries. It means that at last, after 20 centuries, the Jews will begin the work of re-establishing their ancient Homeland, under a stable and civilized Government. The Wandering Jews will at last have a home.

The Jews have always desired to be under British trusteeship, realizing that the British colonizing methods are based upon the notion of giving free scope to the peoples under British protection. The Zionist leaders at San Remo who have been the spokesmen of the Jewish claims are Dr. Weizmann and Mr. Sokolow. They have been greatly assisted by the support of Mr. Herbert Samuel in this country and of Mr. Justice Brandeis in America.

Another factor which undoubtedly contributed to the granting of the Zionist demands is their great moderation.

The practical consequence of the decision at San Remo will be that Jewish energy and capital will begin to flow towards Palestine to be devoted to the development of the country and to the benefit of all its inhabitants.

The event will be celebrated in all Jewish centres with great joy, and the date—April 24, 1920—will perhaps become a Jewish national holiday. A Zionist Congress, and possibly a Pan-Jewish Congress, will have to be convoked at an early date to concentrate Jewish effort on the restoration of Palestine.—*Reuter.*

Article from The Times newspaper, 26 April 1920

26

Palestinians were horrified by Balfour's Declaration. Most Palestinians today would point to Balfour as the root cause for their one hundred years' oppression. The Balfour Declaration represents the height of British imperial arrogance. It took for granted Britain's right, as an imperial power, to control a territory and a people as it saw fit, even before it had any practical or legal control over that territory. Neither the local Arabs in Palestine, nor the small Jewish community living among them, were consulted before Britain promised to create a new Jewish homeland through mass immigration. Palestinians were not offered any representative government. Palestine became yet another British colony, to be used to serve British interests, which at the time aligned with those of Jewish Zionists.

'Lloyd George, to my delight, had forgotten my presence and began to think aloud. Mesopotamia… yes…oil…irrigation…we must have Mesopotamia; Palestine…yes…the Holy Land…Zionism…we must have Palestine; Syria…h'm…what is there in Syria? Let the French have that.'

Lloyd George at the Paris Peace Conferences of 1991, overheard by British delegate Arnold Toynbee

British troops marching past Barclays Bank, Jerusalem, 1938

Britain had welcomed Jewish refugees after the first wave of pogroms in Russia, but by the early 1900s there was a popular backlash against any more Jewish immigration. This phenomenon was repeated in the USA in the early 1920s. Clearly another solution to the persecution of the Jews was needed. British leaders were sympathetic to the plight of the Jews and so they began to look for other creative solutions. The result was the idea of a national home in Palestine, where Jews could live and practise their religion and customs without any fear of persecution.

Map showing Jewish emigration from Europe, 1885-1925

Persecution of the Jews in Russia: a drawing of street riots in Kiev by Oskar E. Wycinek published in German newspaper, Neue Illustrirte Zeitung, 1881

The Balfour Declaration only reflected the wishes of a specific group of Jews, not the whole worldwide Jewish community. For example, of the two British Jews who were cabinet ministers, Herbert Samuel supported the establishment of a national homeland, while his cousin Edwin Montagu was dead against it on the grounds that it would be detrimental to the interests of Jews successfully assimilated in other countries. Zionism was not a position held by all, or even necessarily a majority of Jews. Many agreed with Montagu, that having their own homeland might encourage the persecution of Jews living in other countries.

An election poster for the General Jewish Labour Bund, hung in Kiev, 1917. Written in the Hebrew alphabet, the title reads "Where we live, there is our country!" and the bottom lines "A democratic republic! Full national and political rights for Jews!"

'I wish to place on record my view that the policy of His Majesty's Government is anti-Semitic and in result will prove a rallying ground for Anti-Semites in every country in the world. This view is prompted by the receipt yesterday of a correspondence between Lord Rothschild and Mr. Balfour...I lay down with emphasis four principles:

1. I assert that there is not a Jewish nation. The members of my family, for instance, who have been in this country for generations, have no sort or kind of community of view or of desire with any Jewish family in any other country beyond the fact that they profess to a greater or less degree the same religion. It is no more true to say that a Jewish Englishman and a Jewish Moor are of the same nation than it is to say that a Christian Englishman and a Christian Frenchman are of the same nation...

2. When the Jews are told that Palestine is their national home, every country will immediately desire to get rid of its Jewish citizens, and you will find a population in Palestine driving out its present inhabitants, taking all the best in the country, drawn from all quarters of the globe, speaking every language on the face of the earth, and incapable of communicating with one another except by means of an interpreter...

3. I deny that Palestine is to-day associated with the Jews or properly to be regarded as a fit place for them to live in. The Ten Commandments were delivered to the Jews on Sinai. It is quite true that Palestine plays a large part in Jewish history, but so it does in modern Mahommendan history, and, after the time of the Jews, surely it plays a larger part than any other country in Christian history...

4. ...When the Jew has a national home, surely it follows that the impetus to deprive us of the rights of British citizenship must be enormously increased. Palestine will become the world's Ghetto. Why should the Russian give the Jew equal rights? His national home is Palestine.'

Extracts from a Memorandum of Edwin Montagu, a British Jew and Secretary of State for India, to the British Cabinet, August 1917

29

By the nineteenth century, the majority of Jews in the world lived inside the Russian Empire. From the 1880s they were heavily persecuted and faced regular pogroms. Unsurprisingly, many Jews chose to leave the Russian Empire and seek sanctuary in Western Europe, the USA, and in Palestine. The British took on the humanitarian responsibility of finding a home for Jewish refugees. Palestine was chosen because Jews had ancient religious and cultural roots there and a tradition of immigration. As such, the Balfour Declaration reflected Britain's humanitarian impulses and wish that Jews should be allowed choice in where they settled.

'I am directed by Dr Herzl to convey to your Lordship on behalf of the Zionist Congress which closed last week, the deep and heartfelt thanks of the Congress to His Majesty's Government for the offer....in respect to the proposed Jewish settlement in British East Africa...'

Letter from the World Zionist Organisation to the British Foreign Secretary regarding the offer of land in East Africa, 4 September 1903

Cartoon of Theodore Roosevelt demanding that the Emperor of Russia, Nicholas II, stop oppressing Jews. From Judge Magazine, September 1905, USA

The idea that Jews have a disproportionate influence on global politics is a well-worn anti-Semitic trope. It is often a key part of conspiracy theories, from the early 20th century up to the present day. The motivation for the Balfour Declaration reflects this prejudice. The British thought that by making a concession to Zionist Jews, they would in turn use their power to change US policy in Britain's favour. Britain hoped the Zionists could persuade President Woodrow Wilson to speed up the mobilization of American troops allocated for the British sector of the Western Front in World War I.

'They are a dangerous people to quarrel with, but they are a very helpful people if you can get them on your side,...They are a very subtle race and they have means of communicating throughout the world which nobody seems to know about...

...We had every reason at that time to believe that in both countries the friendliness or hostility of the Jewish race might make a considerable difference,... Jewish propaganda in Russia had a great deal to do with the difficulties created for the Germans in Southern Russia,...The Jews in their subtle way managed to place every obstacle in the way of the Germans... The Zionist movement was exceptionally strong in Russia and America.'

Former Prime Minister Lloyd George describes his attitude to the Jewish people in his witness statement to the Palestine Royal Commission 1936-7

THE STRANGER AT OUR GATE.
EMIGRANT. Can I come in? UNCLE SAM. I 'spose you can; there's no law to keep you out.

Cartoon titled 'Stranger at our Gate' by Frank Beard in 1890 depicting a Jewish immigrant to the US.

The British fulfilled their promise to Sherif Hussein, an Arab leader, to create a new Arab state through the creation of Transjordan. The RAF provided much needed protection to this new country and Hussein's descendants continue to rule Jordan today. It is true that the British were ambiguous about the future status of the land west of Jerusalem when they made their agreement with the Arabs. However, this was not part of an anti-Arab plan. Rather it reflected that the outcome of World War I was still in the balance, and there was no time to iron out every detail of the post-war settlement in the Middle East before securing the support of the Arabs against the Ottomans.

'Whatever may be thought of our case as based on the exact wording of the McMahon letter, it will probably be agreed that, on a broad view of the position, we have an effective answer to Arab criticism. What we promised was to promote Arab independence throughout a wide area. That promise we have substantially fulfilled. Hussein reigns as an independent sovereign at Mecca; Feisal rules at Baghdad; Abdullah in Trans-Jordan. Ibn Saud through his vast territories is free from all fear of Turkish interference or aggression. Further south, the Imam in the Yemen and the Idrisi in Asir rule over independent States. The Arabs as a whole have acquired a freedom undreamed of before the war. Considering what they owe to us, they may surely let us have our way in one small area, which we do not admit to be covered by our pledges, and which in any case, for historical and other reasons, stands on a wholly different footing from the rest of the Arab countries.'

Memorandum by the British Secretary of State for the Colonies, 11 February 1923

Meeting between Amir Abdullah ibn Hussein and British High Commissioner Herbert Samuel in Amman, Jordan, April 1921. During these meetings British High Commissioner Herbert Samuel proclaimed Amir Abdullah the ruler of Transjordan, under British protection

Between 1916 and 1917, the British government knowingly entered three contradictory agreements about what would happen in the event of an Allied victory. Sir Henry McMahon, in a series of letters to Sharif Hussein, promised the Arabs self-government in return for an Arab revolt against the Ottomans, Balfour promised the Jews a national homeland in Palestine, and behind everyone's backs, Mark Sykes and Georges Picot carved up the area into spheres of French and British control and influence. Britain was willing to lie to all sides to gain what it wanted: a new colony to do with as it saw fit.

October 24 1915

1. Subject to the above modifications, Great Britain is prepared to recognize and support the independence of the Arabs in all the regions within the limits demanded by the Sherif of Mecca.

2. Great Britain will guarantee the Holy Places against all external aggression and will recognise their inviolability.

3. When the situation admits, Great Britain will give to the Arabs her advice and will assist them to establish what may appear to be the most suitable forms of government in those various territories.

I am convinced that this declaration will assure you beyond all possible doubt of the sympathy of Great Britain towards the aspirations of her friends the Arabs and will result in a firm and lasting alliance, the immediate results of which will be the expulsion of the Turks from the Arab countries and the freeing of the Arab peoples from the Turkish yoke, which for so many years has pressed heavily upon them.

A. H. Mcmahon
A Mcmahon

Letter from A.H. McMahon to Hussein bin Ali, Sharif of Mecca, 24 October 1915. Part of the McMahon-Hussein correspondence

'As you know I have all along been a strong advocate of being as open as possible with the Sharif [Hussein]. My considered opinion is that we have not been as open and frank as we should been at this last meeting.

Special representatives of Great Britain and France came expressly to fix things up with the Sharif and when the latter agreed to France having the same status in Syria as we are to have in Iraq surely the main points of our agreement re Iraq should have been stated to prevent all chance of a misunderstanding which might have far reaching consequences...If the Sharif puts one construction on McMahon's letter and we another, there is likely to serious trouble.

...we have not played a straight forward game with a courteous old man who is, as Sykes agrees, one of Great Britain's most sincere and loyal admirers.... If we are not going to see the Sharif through, and we let him down badly after all his trust in us, the very 'enviable' post of Pilgrimage Officer at Jeddah will be vacant because I certainly could not remain.'

Letter from Colonel Cyril Wilson, the main liaison with King Hussein to British authorities in Cairo, 24 May 1917

The British government was forced to play a difficult balancing act. Given the circumstances, Britain was remarkably even-handed. In the Balfour Declaration, the British were careful to emphasize the civil and religious rights of the existing non-Jewish communities in Palestine. They were also aware that increased rights for Jews in Palestine should not become an excuse for fewer rights for Jews elsewhere. The British also tried to limit Jewish immigration so that it did not exceed Palestine's 'absorptive capacity'. These efforts demonstrate that Britain intended to pursue a sustainable solution in Palestine, one which could have worked for both Arabs and Jews.

'Unauthorized statements have been made to the effect that the purpose in view is to create a wholly Jewish Palestine. Phrases have been used such as that Palestine is to become 'as Jewish as England is English.' His Majesty's Government regard any such expectation as impracticable, and have no such aim in view. Nor have they at any time contemplated, as appears to be feared by the Arab Delegation, the disappearance or the subordination of the Arabic population, language or culture in Palestine. They would draw attention to the fact that the terms of the Declaration referred to do not contemplate that Palestine as a whole should be converted into a Jewish National Home, but that such a Home should be founded in Palestine. ... For the fulfilment of this policy it is necessary that the Jewish community in Palestine should be able to increase its numbers by immigration. This immigration cannot be so great in volume as to exceed whatever may be the economic capacity of the country at the time to absorb new arrivals. It is essential to ensure that the immigrants should not be a burden upon the people of Palestine as a whole, and that they should not deprive any section of the present population of their employment.'

Extract from the 1939 White Paper, issued by the British in response to the 1936–1939 Arab revolt in Palestine

Coins issued during the British Mandate, with writing in English, Arabic and Hebrew

The Balfour Declaration failed to protect the rights of the vast majority of Arab Muslims and Christians whose communities had been living in Palestine for more than a thousand years. The Arabs are not even mentioned by name, and it's notable that while the Declaration says that 'nothing shall be done which may prejudice the civil and religious rights of existing non-Jewish communities in Palestine', there is no mention of their political or economic rights. Without these rights, the Palestinians were not treated as citizens. They had no way of opposing or even informing British policy for Palestine which was decided in London.

'There arises the further question, what is to become of the people of this country, assuming the Turk to be expelled, and the inhabitants not to have been exterminated by the war ? There are over half a million of these, Syrian Arabs—a mixed community with Arab, Hebrew, Canaanite, Greek, Egyptian, and possibly Crusaders' blood. They and their forefathers have occupied the country for the best part of 1,500 years. They own the soil, which belongs either to individual landowners or to village communities. They profess the Mohammedan faith. They will not be content either to be expropriated for Jewish immigrants, or to act merely as hewers of wood and drawers of water to the latter.'

Cabinet Memorandum 'The Future of Palestine' by Lord Curzon, October 1917

A political cartoon published in the Palestinian newspaper 'Falastin', 1936

35

The Balfour Declaration was a British attempt to establish a homeland for the Jews, where they could be free of persecution. The later events of the Holocaust proved that those who supported this idea were incontrovertibly in the right. Had the British rejected Zionism and tried to settle Jewish refugees in Western Europe, even more Jews would have been killed by the Nazis. The Balfour Declaration showed British foresight in trying to find a solution for the persecution of Jews in Europe. And it should be remembered they did this at a time when the Holocaust appeared inconceivable.

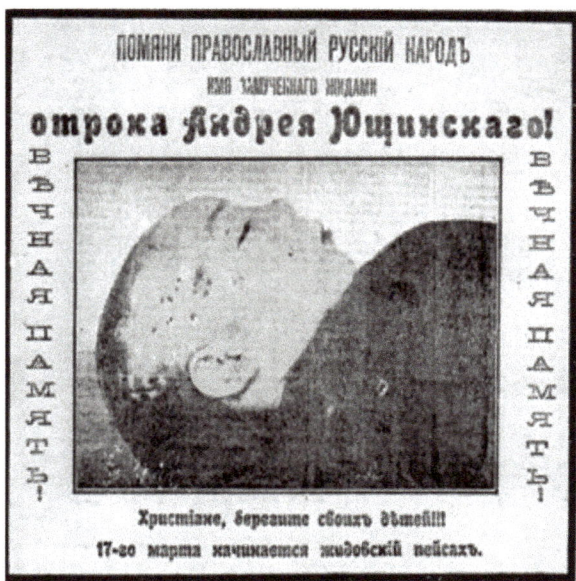

In 1913, Menahem Mendel Beilis, a Russian Jew, was accused of the ritual murder of a 13-year old boy in Kyiv, then part of the Russian Empire. During the trial, these anti-Semitic fliers were distributed in Kyiv. They read 'Orthodox Russian people, commemorate the name of the youth Andriy Yushchinskyi who was martyred by Zhids! Memory eternal to him! Christians, guard your children!!! On March 17, the passover of the Zhids [an ethnic slur for Jews] begins.' Beilis was eventually acquitted

The caption to the photo reads: 'Thousands of Jews marched in the great New York Parade to a mass meeting of protest against recent pogroms in Ukraine, where, speakers said, 120,000 Jews have been massacred. In the parade a service flag was carried with 8,000 stars for Jews killed in service of the United States.' Article from the Oklahoma newspaper the Ardmoreite, 2 December 1919

36

The Balfour Declaration's promise to create a homeland for the Jews in the Middle East was a major mistake. Its promise of a Jewish homeland did not prevent the Holocaust nor did it lead to peace afterwards. In fact, the creation of the state of Israel has been one of the primary causes of wars in the Middle East. Additionally, less than half of the world's Jews have chosen to live there, so Israel has not become a true Jewish homeland, but a militaristic ethno-religious state in which Arabs are either second class citizens or denied citizenship.

'In the period of over two years since the establishment of the office, conditions in Germany which created refugees have developed so catastrophically that a reconsideration by the League of Nations of the entire situation is essential....tens of thousands are to-day anxiously seeking ways to flee abroad....and the doors of most countries are closed against impoverished fugitives....Efforts must be made to remove or mitigate the causes which create German refugees....The moral authority of the League of Nations and of the States Members of the League must be directed towards a determined appeal to the German Government in the name of humanity and of the principles of the public law in Europe.'

Letter of resignation of James G. McDonald, the League of Nations' High Commissioner for Refugees (Jewish and other) coming from Germany, 27 December 1935

Map of major deportations to Auschwitz from Europe by the end of 1942

37

CHAPTER 3

The British Mandate

Should the British Government be praised or blamed for its management of the Mandate in Palestine?

Britain opened the Mandate's borders so Jews fleeing persecution could be safe in their historic homeland. It did so by calculating Palestine's capacity to absorb refugees and kept Jewish immigration within those limits. Given the numbers of Jewish refugees fleeing persecution, it was impossible for the British to argue that Palestine should not receive any Jews, especially because there was an existing Jewish community as well as a historic connection to the land.

The SS Tiger Hill carrying illegal Jewish immigrants was intercepted and fired on by Royal Navy gunboats off Tel Aviv in September 1939

Supplement No. 2
to
The Palestine Gazette No. 1506 of 18th July, 1946.

IMMIGRATION ORDINANCE, 1941.
ORDER BY THE HIGH COMMISSIONER.

IN VIRTUE of the powers conferred on the High Commissioner by section 5(3) of the Immigration Ordinance, 1941, His Excellency is pleased to order, and it is hereby ordered, as follows: No. 5 of 1941.

The maximum aggregate number of immigration certificates in all categories that may be granted during the period from the 15th July, 1946 to the 14th August, 1946, shall be 1,600.

No immigration certificate issued during this period shall be valid for the admission of more than one person.

By His Excellency's Command,

J. V. W. SHAW
Chief Secretary.

12th July, 1946.

EXPLANATORY NOTE.

The quota prescribed above provides for the issue of immigration certificates for Palestine during the month beginning on the 15th July and ending on the 14th August, 1946.

Of the number prescribed 100 are for Arab and other immigrants and 1,500 for Jewish immigrants.

Document restricting the number of immigration passes to be issued into Palestine. Issued by the British government in 1939

40

When Britain took over the running of Palestine, relations between the long-established Jewish community and other religions was harmonious. By the time the British left in 1948 Arabs and Jews were fighting a civil war. The League of Nations had awarded the British Government the Mandate to safeguard the rights of all inhabitants of Palestine and prepare the territory for self-government. But when the British took over from the Ottomans, they made no serious attempts to create consensus between the Arabs and the Zionists in Palestine and so helped to create the conditions for sectarian violence. By leaving Palestine in a civil war, Britain completely failed to uphold its Mandate.

'Musa recalls that the child who became his own foster-brother was the son of the Jewish grocer down the street, and that for the next thirty years the two families used to visit each other, to exchange presents on each other's feast days, and to proffer congratulations or condolences as occasions demanded.'

Extract from Geoffrey Furlonge, 'Palestine is my Country - the Story of Musa Alami'. Alami recalled his childhood growing up in Palestine before the British mandate

'We consider every Jew to be armed...no Jewish individual, or home or settlement is free from such arms which are intended to fight the Arabs and destroy them. This situation suggests to every Arab that he must be ready to defend himself and should arm himself, and should not remain defenceless before his armed opponent.'

Resolution of a meeting of Palestinians at Nablus on the 19th Anniversary of the Balfour Declaration, 2 November 1935

Both the Arab and the Jewish positions were completely maximalist. Neither side was prepared to make any compromise or accommodation with the other. Britain made efforts to find a peaceful and collaborative settlement, including, for example, a shared council representing all communities to solve practical issues together. The animosity between Jews and Arabs meant that British attempts at peaceful, sustainable government were always destined to come to nothing. Given this intransigence there was little Britain could do other than try to keep the peace.

(Above) Jewish protest against the 1939 White Paper, (below) Palestinian Arabs at Abou Ghosh taking the oath of allegiance to the Arab cause including to fight Jewish immigration

V.—The Problem Referred to the United Nations

After the failure of these discussions His Majesty's Government decided that the only course now open to them was to submit the problem to the judgment of the United Nations, asking that body to recommend a solution. The reasons for this decision were explained by His Majesty's Principal Secretary of State for Foreign Affairs in a speech to the House of Commons on 18th February, 1947, in which he said:—

"His Majesty's Government have been faced with an irreconcilable conflict of principles. There are in Palestine about 1,200,000 Arabs and 600,000 Jews. For the Jews the essential point of principle is the creation of a sovereign Jewish State. For the Arabs, the essential point of principle is to resist to the last the establishment of Jewish sovereignty in any part of Palestine. The discussions of the last month have quite clearly shown that there is no prospect of resolving this conflict by any settlement negotiated between the parties. But if the conflict has to be resolved by an arbitrary decision, that is not a decision which His Majesty's Government are empowered, as Mandatory, to take. His Majesty's Government have of themselves no power, under the terms of the Mandate, to award the country either to the Arabs or to the Jews, or even to partition it between them."

Extract from the official termination of the British Mandate, 15 May 1948

British policy in Palestine always favoured the Jews. The first High Commissioner to Palestine appointed by the British Government was Sir Herbert Samuel, a keen British Zionist. While in public the British continued to pay lip service to Arab aspirations for a state of their own, they also committed to creating a Jewish national homeland in Palestine. Not only did the British fail their Mandate to prepare Palestine for self-government, but they also left the Arabs with fewer democratic rights than they had under the Ottomans.

Telegram to the General Peace Conference in Paris.

All the inhabitants of Palestine consisting of the Arab Districts of Jerusalem, Nablus and Acre, both Moslems and Christians, have assembled together and selected their delegates, who came and held a general meeting in Jerusalem to discuss the form of the Government suitable to their country.

They have decided before entering into any discussion on the subject, first of all to submit to your Supreme Conference their strong protest owing to what they have heard that the Zionists have been promised to have our own country as their own National one; that they intend to immigrate to this country and to colonize it.

Therefore we the assembled Moslems and Christians as delegates for an alive Arab Nation, included amongst the weak Nations liberated by the Allies, do hereby utterly refuse every decision which may be given in this connexion before taking our opinion.

We are submitting to the Conference a detailed statement of the prejudice which will be caused to the interests of the inhabitants of this country, both Moslem and Christian, who form the absolute majority, owing to the Zionists immigration and colonization in this country, and their making it their National abode.

We request your Supreme Conference not to give any decision regarding this country except after receiving our wishes and aspirations which shall be submitted.

Jerusalem,

3rd February, 1919.

Telegram of protest against Zionism from the Jaffa Muslim Christian Committee to Prime Minister Lloyd George at the 1919 Paris Peace Conference

'On the strength of our word the Jews have come to Palestine and established their national home there: it would surely be one of the greatest betrayals in history to abandon them now to their fate as a minority in an independent Arab state. Nor is it to be expected that the Jews, whose strength is already one third in population and predominant in wealth, will ever agree to subordinate their progressive modern "European" community to the domination of a relatively backward Arab majority whom (in some respects justly) they despise.'

John Martin, Assistant Under-Secretary at the Colonial Office writing to Sir Henry Gurney, Chief Secretary in Jerusalem, January 1947

Maintaining the Mandate was a burden that Britain shouldered, and it cost the country dearly in money and lives. Many people from Britain served in Palestine, as administrators, policemen or armed forces. These duties were sometimes difficult and dangerous; nearly 200 military personnel were killed during the Arab Uprising of 1936-1939, and between 1944 and the end of the Mandate on May 14, 1948, 228 police, soldiers and administrators were killed. It was only through the sacrifices made by British forces that major violence between Jews and Arabs was prevented during the Mandate. It is not a coincidence that civil war broke out immediately after the British departed.

A British military funeral in Palestine, 1946

Officers of The Loyal Regiment (North Lancashire) next to a railway wagon. They were engaged in rail protection duties against militant Arab groups opposed to the British Mandate and illegal Jewish immigration

It was natural that the Arabs, frustrated by the broken promises of the British and alarmed by increasing numbers of Jewish immigrants arriving, should organise themselves against British rule. However, the British did little to defuse the unrest in 1929 or 1936 before it became violent. Instead, they relied on tactics perfected over decades of colonial administration around the world. They brutally suppressed unrest, killed large numbers of Palestinian rebels, and exiled a generation of Palestinian political leaders.

British soldiers on an armoured train car with two Palestinian hostages as human shields, 1936

Palestinians swear an oath of allegiance to the nationalist cause in 1936

45

At the end of World War II Britain was almost bankrupt, having spent all its national resources in its fight against the Nazis. The country now relied on loans from the American government to stay afloat. The British were forced to leave Palestine when the US government withdrew its support and insisted on increasing levels of Jewish immigration. The British knew this was a mistake which would make a peaceful settlement between Arabs and Jews impossible. But Britain was now too indebted to the USA to fight American decisions on Palestine. The British had to concede or face financial ruin.

British propaganda poster designed to raise money from the public for the war effort through war savings, 1944

MY DEAR MR. PRIME MINISTER:

...It appears that the available certificates for immigration to Palestine will be exhausted in the near future. It is suggested that the granting of an additional one hundred thousand of such certificates would contribute greatly to a sound solution for the future of Jews still in Germany and Austria, and for other Jewish refugees...the American people firmly believe that immigration into Palestine should not be closed...The main solution appears to lie in the quick evacuation of as many as possible of the non-repatriable Jews, who wish it, to Palestine. If it is to be effective, such action should not be long delayed.

Very sincerely yours,

Harry S. Truman

Letter from US President Truman to Prime Minister Winston Churchill, 31 August 1945

In February 1947 the British simply gave up the political fight to find a solution to deteriorating relations between Jews and Arabs in Palestine. Britain deserves no praise for handing the problem of Palestine over to the United Nations. The British were simply washing their hands of what they thought was an impossible situation. When the UN voted on Resolution 181 establishing Israel as a state for Jews, Britain, although it knew this was unfair on Arabs, was too cowardly to take a position, and simply abstained. The USA and USSR were therefore able to force through the establishment of Israel.

IV.—The Obstacles which Frustrated the Efforts of His Majesty's Government to Establish Self-Governing Institutions in Palestine

The Government of Palestine were unable to make comparable progress towards the accomplishment of their third task, the preparation of the people for self-government, owing to the mutual hostility of Arabs and Jews. The existence of Arab opposition to the creation of a Jewish national home was apparent even before the Mandate began. The American King-Crane Commission sent out to the Middle East by President Wilson in 1919 had reported that:

"The Peace Conference should not shut its eyes to the fact that the anti-Zionist feeling in Palestine and Syria is intense and not lightly to be flouted. No British officer, consulted by the Commissioners, believed that the Zionist programme could be carried out except by force of arms."

Extract from the official termination of the British Mandate, 15 May 1948

The departure of the British from Haifa, 30 June 1948

47

It was unfair that Britain was painted as the villain at the time because it was Britain that had lost troops and spent money on keeping the peace in Palestine. Neither the USA nor the USSR in the United Nations was interested in helping Britain maintain peace and both superpowers favoured Jewish claims to the land. While the USA and the USSR took the moral high ground against British imperialism, their motives were less noble. Both the USA and the USSR enjoyed seeing their rival, the British Empire, humiliated. Neither of these huge countries wanted to accept post-war Jewish refugees themselves.

'.....the average American supported immigration to Palestine simply because he did not want more Jews in America.....By shouting for a Jewish state, Americans satisfy many motives. They are attacking the Empire and British protectionism, they are espousing a moral cause, for whose fulfilment they will take no responsibility, and most important of all, they are diverting attention from the fact that their own immigration laws are one of the causes of the problem.'

Extract from 'Palestine Mission. A Personal Record', 1947 by British Labour MP Richard Crossman, member of the Anglo American Committee on Palestine

A lorry bearing the faces of past and current Soviet Communist leaders Lenin and Stalin parading through Tel Aviv on International Labour Day, 1 May 1949

48

British administration across its possessions was often pragmatic, short-sighted, and self-serving. In the 1920s British administrators simply refused to live up to all the promises they had made to the Arabs, and in the 1940s they lacked the moral vision to fashion the right response to the unique horror of the Holocaust. When the British withdrew in 1947, the government acted under pressure from the British public, who did not want to see more British lives lost far away in Palestine. As ever, Britain put its own interests first, and those of its colonies and dependencies, firmly second.

'I am assured that the solution of the problem of Palestine which would be most welcome to the leaders and supporters of the Zionist movement throughout the world would be the annexation of the country to the British Empire...

It is hoped that under British rule facilities would be given to Jewish organisations to purchase land, to found colonies, to establish educational and religious institutions, and to spend usefully the funds that would be freely contributed for promoting the economic development of the country....

From the standpoint of British interests there are several arguments for this policy, if wider considerations should allow it to be pursued:-

1. It would enable England to fulfil in yet another sphere her historic part of civiliser of the backward countries....

2. The British Empire, with its present vastness and prosperity, has little addition to its greatness left to win. But Palestine, small as it is in area, bulks so large in the world's imagination, that no Empire is so great but its prestige would be raised by its possession. The inclusion of Palestine within the British Empire would add a lustre even to the British Crown....

3. ....if Great Britain can obtain the compensations, which public opinion will demand, in Mesopotamia and Palestine and not in German East Africa and West Africa, there is more likelihood of a lasting peace....'

Extract from 'The Future of Palestine', also known as the Samuel memorandum, circulated by Jewish MP Herbert Samuel to the British Cabinet in January and March 1915

"This is a lamentable situation. However we may differ, it is one of the most unhappy, unpleasant situations into which we have got, even in these troublous years. Here, we are expending hard earned money at an enormous rate in Palestine. Everyone knows what our financial difficulties are-how heavy the weight of taxation. We are spending a vast sum of money on this business. For 18 months we have been pouring out our wealth on this unhappy, unfortunate and discreditable business. Then there is the manpower of at least 100,000 men in Palestine, who might well be at home strengthening our depleted industry. What are they doing there? What good are we getting out of it?

We are told that there are a handful of terrorists on one side and 100,000 British troops on the other. How much does it cost? No doubt it is £300 a year per soldier in Palestine. That is apart from what I call a slice of the overheads, which is enormous, of the War Office and other Services. That is £30 million a year. It may be much more between £30 million and £40 million a year which is being poured out and which would do much to help to find employment in these islands, or could be allowed to return to fructify in the pockets of the people.'

Speech on Palestine by Winston Churchill in the House of Commons, 31 January 1947

CHAPTER 4

The Israeli War of Independence / Palestinian Nakba 1948

What caused the dispossession of the majority of Arab Palestinians from their home?

Palestinians were only dispossessed because there was a war. This war was started by Palestinian leaders, who rejected the UN Partition Plan without any idea of how to resist it. While the Jews accepted the UN Partition Plan, the Palestinian leadership voted to call a three-day labour strike. This descended into rioting, attacks on Jewish properties, and ultimately a war for which the Palestinians were poorly prepared. Many Palestinians expected a large-scale invasion by Arab states to support them, nor did Palestinian leaders caution their followers against using violence. In these circumstances, Jews were drawn into a war. They didn't expect to win it so comprehensively and they can't be blamed for doing so.

Aftermath of attacks on the Jewish Commercial Quarter in Jerusalem on 2nd December 1947, a few days after the positive vote at the UN on the Partition Plan for Palestine

'The blood will flow like rivers in the Middle East,' promised Jamal Husseini, [secretary to the Executive Committee of the Palestine Arab Congress (1921-1934) and to the Muslim Supreme Council]...Arab politicians had warned that 'if a satisfactory solution of the Palestine case was not reached, severe measures should be taken against all Jews in Arab countries.'

Iraqi Prime Minister Nuri al-Said: 'We will smash the country (Israel) with our guns and obliterate every place the Jews seek shelter in.'

Quotes from Arab leaders in response to the UN Partition Plan of 1947

The forced dispossession of over half the Arab population from their homes was the culmination of the long-held Zionist ambition to found a Jewish state in Palestine. Palestinians wanted and had been promised an independent state of their own, and they accepted that a small Jewish community could continue to live in this state as a protected minority, as it always had done. From the very start Zionist leaders knew that their slogan 'Palestine is a land without a people for a people without a land' was nonsense and the land which would become Israel would have to be taken from Arabs. They used a range of methods from land purchase to terror attacks, to all-out war, to force Palestinians off the land.

A future Israeli Prime Minister Menachem Begin giving a speech in Tel Aviv, 14th August 1948. Note the map of Greater Israel in front of him

'It must be clear that there is no room in the country for both peoples... If the Arabs leave it, the country will become wide and spacious for us... The only solution is a Land of Israel... without Arabs. There is no room here for compromises... There is no way but to transfer the Arabs from here to the neighbouring countries, and to transfer all of them... For this goal funds will be found... And only after this transfer will the country be able to absorb millions of our brothers and the Jewish problem will cease to exist.'

Joseph Weitz, a director of the Jewish National Fund, wrote this extract in his diary on 20 December 1940

53

Palestinian leaders urged Palestinians to leave their homes to clear the way for Arab troops to fight Israeli soldiers and minimise Palestinian civilian casualties. But they gravely underestimated the Israeli army and overestimated the armies of Egypt, Syria and Jordan which were soundly defeated. After the war, it was unrealistic to expect the new state of Israel to open its borders to Palestinians who had left in the hope that the Jews would be driven out of Palestine. It was inconceivable that these defeated Palestinians would want to become citizens of the state of Israel. And in reality, war had solved some demographic problems which the mapmakers had never done satisfactorily for either side.

```
                                    District Police Headquarters
                                    (C.I.D.)
                                    P.O.B. 700.
                                    Haifa.
                                    26th April, 1948.

S E C R E T
A/A.I.G.  C.I.D.

Subject:-          General Situation Haifa District.

Haifa remains quiet. Yesterday produced a noticeable change in the general
atmosphere and businesses and shops in the lower town were open for the first time
in many days. Traffic started to move normally around the town and people
returning to the places of business filled the streets. In fact, Haifa presented a
more normal appearance than it had done for a long while. Some Arabs were seen
moving among the Jews in the lower town and German Colony area and these were
allowed free and unmolested passage. An appeal has been made to the Arabs by the
Jews to reopen their shops and businesses in order to relieve the difficulties of
feeding the Arab population. Evacuation was still going on yesterday and several
trips were made by 'Z' craft to Acre. Roads too, were crowded with people leaving
Haifa with all their belongings. At a meeting yesterday afternoon Arab leaders
reiterated their determination to evacuate the entire Arab population and they
have been given the loan of ten 3-ton military trucks as from this morning to
assist the evacuation.

                        * * *

(A.J. Bidmead.)
for SUPERINTENDENT OF POLICE

Copy:-.District Commissioner, Haifa
Superintendent of Police, Haifa
File
```

British police report on the Arab evacuation of Haifa

'Only an extremely small, almost insignificant number of the refugees during this early period left because of Haganah or IZL or LHI expulsion orders or forceful "advice" to that effect. Many more – especially women, children and old people – left as a result of orders or advice from Arab military commanders and officials. Fears for their safety rather than a grand strategy of evacuation underlay these steps.'

Extract from 'The Birth of the Palestinian Refugee Problem Revisited' by B.Morris (2004), Cambridge University Press, p.139

54

After 1945, the British were the only control and limit on mass Jewish immigration, which is why the Jews turned against them. Armed Jewish groups, quickly identified as 'terrorists' by the British, blew up railway lines, mined roads, sabotaged oil pipelines, and bombed the King David Hotel, (the British HQ in Jerusalem) killing 91 people. Exhausted by World War II and pressurised by US politicians, Britain handed the question of Palestine to the United Nations. The Zionists' terrorism was rewarded – the UN Partition Plan gave them over half the land on the assumption that mass Jewish immigration was unstoppable. This led of course to war, and from there to the expulsion of Palestinians from their ancestral homes.

'During the morning [the Jews] were continually shooting down on all Arabs who moved both in Wadi Nisnas and the Old City. This included completely indiscriminate and revolting machinegun fire, mortar fire and sniping on women and children sheltering in churches and attempting to get out... through the gates into the docks... there was considerable congestion outside the East Gate of hysterical and terrified Arab women and children and old people on whom the Jews opened up mercilessly with fire. Two [Royal Marine] officers were seriously wounded.'

A British intelligence officer's account, 22 April 1948

British Army HQ after it was bombed by the Irgun, a Jewish terrorist group, in 1946

Every war causes refugees to flee their homes. In the shadow of World War II, which had created many millions of 'displaced people' including many Jews, the consequences for Palestinians in 1948 were not unusual. After the Jewish army had defeated the Palestinian army in May 1948, the Palestinians had not only lost their own military, but were caught in the middle of a war between the Jewish army and the invading armies of the Arab states. It was not surprising that many Palestinians chose to leave their homes in order to escape the fighting.

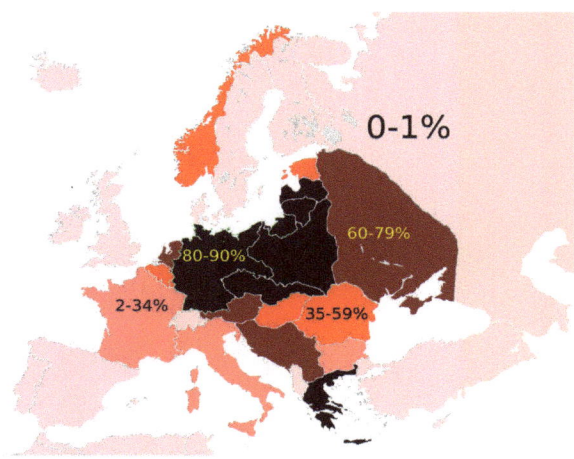

Map of the Jewish Holocaust death toll as a % of the total pre-war Jewish population by country/region

'When the issue of refugees is raised within the context of the Middle East, people invariably refer to Palestinian refugees, not former Jewish refugees from Arab countries. Yet, there were two major population movements that occurred during years of turmoil in the Middle East. In fact, there were more former Jewish refugees uprooted from Arab countries (over 850,000) than there were Palestinians who became refugees in 1948 (UN estimate: 726,000).'

Extract from a report submitted to the European Parliament in 2006 by Justice for Jews from Arab Countries (JJAC), a political advocacy organisation founded in New York in 2002

While the Palestinian leadership still naively expected the British to keep their promises, the Jewish leadership had prepared for a civil war. They had recruited and trained a shadow army, including radical paramilitary groups, called the Irgun and Lehi, who were ready to seize the land for a new state when the British withdrew. It was this army that defeated the Palestinian army in the spring of 1948, leaving the Palestinian population defenceless when war broke out between Israel and the Arab states in May 1948.

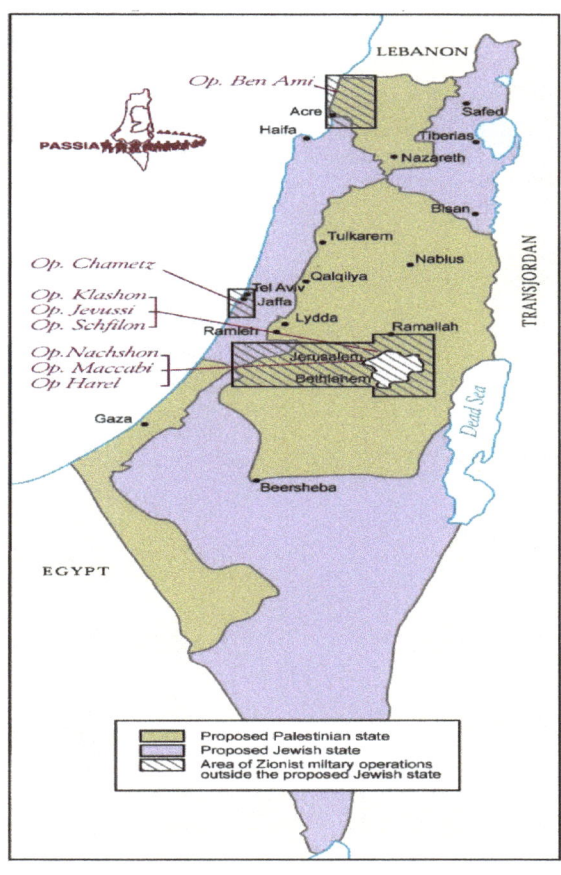

Zionist Military Operations outside the UN-proposed Jewish State, 1 April 1948 - 15 May 1948

' "We adopt the system of aggressive defense; with every Arab attack we must respond with a decisive blow: the destruction of the place or the expulsion of the residents along with the seizure of the place." He declared: "When in action we . . . must fight strongly and cruelly, letting nothing stop us." '

Ben-Gurion's war diaries, on 19 December 1947 quoted in Flapan's 'The Palestinian Exodus of 1948', Journal of Palestinian Studies, 1987 vol 16 number 4

The actions of some Jewish combat units almost certainly did contribute to the Palestinian exodus. But these were the exception, mostly committed by irregular units, and were discouraged by army high command. It was understandable that Jewish fighters would be aggressive. The ranks of the Haganah, the main Zionist armed force, had been swelled by Holocaust survivors who were desperate to fight for the existence of the Jewish people. For them, Arab leaders' promises to push the Jews into the sea echoed the rhetoric of anti-Semitic propaganda from World War II. In some cases, the Haganah's actions actually saved Palestinian lives by clearing civilians from the scene of battle.

Adolf Hitler talking to Palestinian leader Grand Mufti Haj Amin al-Husseini, 28th November 1941

'Sheikh Hassan el-Bana, head of the Moslem Brotherhood, largest of the extremist Arab nationalist organizations, declared in an interview today: "If the Jewish state becomes a fact, and this is realized by the Arab peoples, they will drive the Jews who live in their midst into the sea." '

An extract from the New York Times by Dana Adams Schmidt

In April 1948, the Jewish leadership launched Plan Dalet. This sought to exploit the Palestinians' fragmented and dispersed forces and called for the forced expulsion of civilians who resisted Jewish military control. This plan gave Jewish troops a free rein to decide who was resisting and so who needed expelling. This led to massacres of Palestinians, like that at Deir Yassin, a village near Jerusalem. News of this massacre caused more Palestinians to panic and flee. Israelis covered up this massacre for years. When evidence later emerged, they then claimed it was an aberration committed by irregular troops. Plan Dalet shows that ethnic cleansing had always been part of the plan.

'We have no wish to fight ordinary people who want to live in peace, but only the army and forces which are preparing to invade Palestine. Therefore . . . all people who do not want this war must leave together with their women and children in order to be safe. This is going to be a cruel war, with no mercy or compassion. There is no reason why you should endanger yourselves.'

Translation from Arabic of a leaflet dropped from an aircraft on Arab villages in the Galilee on the orders of the Haganah Command (the Jewish armed force) in 1948

New Palestine Party

Visit of Menachen Begin and Aims of Political Movement Discussed

TO THE EDITOR OF THE NEW YORK TIMES:

Among the most disturbing political phenomena of our time is the emergence in the newly created state of Israel of the "Freedom Party" (Tnuat Haherut), a political party closely akin in its organization, methods, political philosophy and social appeal to the Nazi and Fascist parties. It was formed out of the membership and following of the former Irgun Zvai Leumi, a terrorist, right-wing, chauvinist organization in Palestine.

Extract from a letter 2 December 1948 published in the New York Times from a group of leading Jews based in the US, including Albert Einstein, complaining about a massacre of Arab villagers at Deir Yassin and comparing a new political party, led by future Israeli PM, Menachem Begin, with the Nazis

It is true that in April 1948 Jewish political and military leadership did launch a major military strategy: Plan Dalet, which ordered Jewish troops to expel any Arab civilians who resisted. But this didn't apply to civilians who cooperated with Israeli forces, nor did it apply to Palestinians who lived beyond the areas allocated to the Jews in the UN Partition Plan. In this sense, the Haganah was just enforcing the terms of the internationally agreed UN Partition Plan. That is why there are still 1.7 million Arab Israeli citizens today.

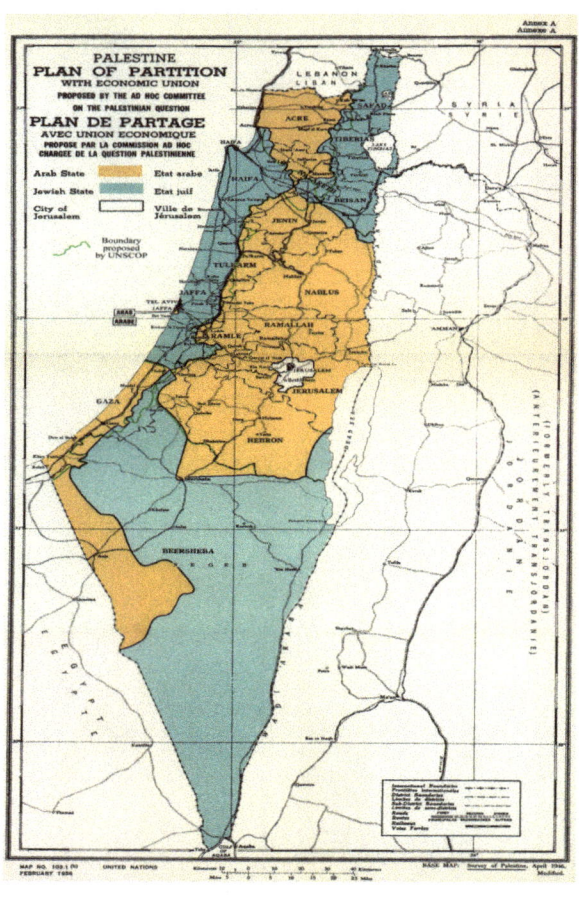

United Nations Partition Plan

'As noted previously, some Arabs certainly were expelled by Jewish troops, as would be expected in a war. However, in most cases, the Jewish forces acted in order to avoid being accused of confiscation. For instance, when Jewish forces seized Tiberias on April 19, 1948, and the entire Arab population of 6,000 was evacuated under British military supervision, the Jewish Community Council issued a statement of clarification: "We did not dispossess them; they themselves chose this course.... Let no citizen touch their property." Likewise, in both Tiberias and Haifa, the Haganah issued orders that none of the Arabs' possessions should be touched, and warned that anyone violating these orders would be severely punished.'

Extract from the New York Times, 1st December 1947, on the decision in the General Assembly of the United Nations to partition Palestine

Israel refused to accept peace agreements with its Arab neighbours because the Arab leaders insisted that Palestinian refugees had the right to return to their homes. Israel did not want the Palestinians it had ethnically cleansed to return. For Palestinians, the years 1948-9 are the Nakba (the disaster) when at least half of their population was forced to leave their homes and become refugees. Millions of Palestinians are still trapped in Lebanon, Syria, and Jordan, as well as semi-permanent refugee camps in the West Bank and Gaza over seventy-five years later.

UNITED NATIONS
Department of Public Information
Press and Publications Bureau
Lake Success, New York

Press Release PAL/537
4 November 1949

200 DISPLACED ARABS RETURN TO THEIR VILLAGE UNDER UN AUSPICES

The return of some 200 Arabs to the native village of Wadi Fukin near Bethlehem yesterday crowned a settlement under United Nations auspices of a three-month dispute between Arabs and Jews.

The dispute arose on 15 July when the Israeli Army expelled the population of Wadi Fukin after the village had been transferred to the Israeli-occupied area under the terms of the Armistice Agreement concluded between Israel and the Jordan Kingdom....

The Mixed Armistice Commission decided on 31 August, by a majority vote, that Israel had violated the Armistice Agreement by expelling villagers across the demarcation line and decided that they should be allowed to return to their homes.

However, when the villagers returned to Wadi Fukin under the supervision of the United Nations observers on September 6, they found most of their houses destroyed and were again compelled by the Israeli Army to return to Arab territory...

UN Press Release on Arabs displaced by Israeli troops

Jaramana Refugee Camp for Palestinians, Damascus, Syria, 1948

61

CHAPTER 5

The Six Day War / the Palestinian Naksa 1967

Was Israel's surprise attack on its neighbours a legitimate defensive strategy?

Israel defeated the surrounding Arab states in its victorious War of Independence in 1948–49. The Arab states wanted revenge. In 1964, their leaders met at the Arab League summit in Cairo. They came up with a plan to disrupt Israel's water supply by diverting water from the Jordan River away from Israel. They also established the Palestinian Liberation Organisation (PLO), which aimed to attack Israel inside its new borders. These moves were part of Arab countries' long-standing and ongoing ambitions to destroy the state of Israel.

'The establishment of Israel is the basic threat that the Arab nation in its entirety has agreed to forestall. And since the existence of Israel is a danger that threatens the Arab nation, the diversion of the Jordan waters by it multiplies the dangers to Arab existence. Accordingly, the Arab states have to prepare the plans necessary for dealing with the political, economic and social aspects, so that if necessary results are not achieved, collective Arab military preparations, when they are not completed, will constitute the ultimate practical means for the final liquidation of Israel.'

Extract from the preamble to the decisions adopted at the 1964 Arab League Summit in Cairo

'The Syrian Army, with its finger on the trigger, is united in the view that the battle must be speedily joined. The time has come to enter into the battle of liberation.'

Statement by Syrian Defence Minister Hafez Assad, 20 May 1967

For Palestinians, the 1967 war is the Naksa (the set back). Many Zionists had wanted Israel's borders to stretch east across the River Jordan and deep into the Sinai in the south. This is why Israel thwarted all attempts at peace agreements after 1948. It never intended to settle its territorial borders along the 1948 armistice lines. It was tactical considerations which dictated the timing of a coordinated attack in June 1967, but if it hadn't been then, it would have been soon. Israel had always planned to go to war again to secure further territorial gains.

Propaganda poster made by the Irgun, a Jewish terrorist organisation active from 1931-48. The map is of Greater Israel, which includes much of Jordan (then the Emirate of Transjordan)

As a bridge is held up by a pillar
As a man is kept erect by his spine
So the Jordan, the holy Jordan
Is the backbone of my Israel.

Two Banks has the Jordan –
This is ours and, that is as well.

Though my country may be poor and small
It is mine from head to foot.
Stretching from the sea to the desert
And the Jordan, the Jordan in the middle.

Two Banks has the Jordan –
This is ours and, that is as well.

From the wealth of our land there shall prosper
The Arab, the Christian, and the Jew,
For our flag is a pure and just one
It will illuminate both sides of my Jordan.

Two Banks has the Jordan –
This is ours and, that is as well.

My two hands I have dedicated to the homeland,
My two hands to sword and shield.
Let my right hand whither
If I forget the East Bank of the Jordan.

Two Banks has the Jordan –
This is ours and, that is as well.'

The poem 'The East Bank of the Jordan' written in 1929 by Zionist leader Ze'ev Jabotinsky

Palestinian terrorists, known as fedayeen, committed 113 attacks inside Israel, launched from their bases in Syria, Egypt, and Jordan, in the months up to May 1967. The Syrian government actively supported and armed a fedayeen leader called Yasser Arafat who led a group called Fatah. He went on to lead armed Palestinian resistance for three decades. The Egyptian government supported another group, the Arab Nationalist Movement. King Hussein of Jordan, while he condemned the attacks that originated in his country, did little to prevent them. In order to stop terrorism, Israel had to move against the countries that sponsored the terrorists.

Plaque in the Negev commemorating Israeli paratroopers who fought Palestinian fedayeen terrorists

Fedayeen marauders killed by Israeli border police after an attack in Nir Galim, 4th September 1956

In November 1966, Israel mobilised 4000-5000 troops and attacked the West Bank village of Samu, killing 16 Jordanian soldiers and three Palestinian civilians, and destroying many Palestinian houses. Jordanians rioted against the King of Jordan because he had failed to protect them from Israel. The revolutionary republics of Egypt and Syria, hoping to gain from Jordan's weakness, called on King Hussein to abdicate. Therefore, Israel attacked Egypt on 5th June 1967, knowing that the cooperation between the armies of Egypt, Syria and Jordan was momentarily at a low ebb.

'Before the June crisis the Arab world could be viewed as divided into two camps. The radical-revolutionary camp comprised the United Arab Republic, Syria, Iraq, Algeria and the Republican regime in war-torn Yemen.

The other Arab camp could be described for want of a better word, as conservative or moderate. It consisted of the five Arab monarchies of Saudi Arabia, Jordan, Libya, Kuwait and Morocco. Definitely anti-revolutionary and bent on preserving their royal establishments.

The struggle between the revolutionary and the conservative camps constituted the essence of Arab politics in the 1950s and 1960s. It overshadowed all other problems, including even that of Arab-Israeli relations.

In the military sector, the most dramatic demonstration of unity was Jordan's plunge into the nearly-suicidal war once Egypt was attacked. By contrast, Syrian action on the front was negligible and showed little evidence of proper synchronization with Egyptian and Jordanian efforts.'

Extract from "Arab Block Realignments" by George Lenczowski, Current History 53, no.316 (1967): 346-84

Aftermath of the Israeli military's attack on Samu, a village in the Jordanian-controlled West Bank, 1967

After Syria's revolution in 1963, the new Syrian government sought to replace Egypt as the leading Arab state by showing the most aggression towards Israel. Israel was geographically vulnerable; it had a very narrow coastal strip and farmlands dominated by a Syrian plateau. In 1966, the Syrian army began firing on Israeli farmers in the demilitarized zone of the Golan Heights. Artillery attacks escalated into aerial battles. Soon, Israeli generals were convinced that this was a precursor to a full-scale attack. They tried to persuade politicians that Israel needed to act soon while it still held an advantage in equipment and particularly in aircraft.

'In August the Syrians opened fire on an Israeli patrol boat that had run aground in the northeastern corner of the Sea of Galilee, and beginning in January 1967, they sporadically attacked patrols and farmers in the DMZ east of the lake. On April 7, the conflict escalated. Both sides used tanks. The IAF bombed and strafed seventeen Syrian positions, and six Syrian MiG-21s were shot down, two of them over Damascus. The Syrians found their inability to stop the flight of Israeli aircraft over their capital particularly humiliating. A few weeks later Syrian intelligence sent an agent using a British passport to set off explosions in Jerusalem during the forthcoming Independence Day celebrations. He was caught before he could do any harm.'

Extract from 'Righteous Victims: A History of the Zionist-Arab Conflict 1881 – 1999' (2002) by Benny Morris, pp.303-4

'2. In pursuance of the spirit of the Security Council resolution of 16 November 1948, the Armistice Demarcation Line and the demilitarized Zone have been defined with a view toward separating the armed forces of the two Parties in such manner as to minimize the possibility of friction and incident, while providing for the gradual restoration of normal civilian life in the area of the Demilitarized Zone, without prejudice to the ultimate settlement.

* * *

4. The armed forces of the two Parties shall nowhere advance beyond the Armistice Demarcation Line.

* * *

5. (a)...the area between the Armistice Demarcation Line and the boundary, pending final territorial settlement between the Parties, shall be established as a Demilitarized Zone from which the armed forces of both Parties shall be totally excluded, and in which no activities by military or para-military forces shall be permitted. This provision applies to the Ein Gev and Dardara sectors which shall form part of the Demilitarized Zone.

(b) Any advance by the armed forces, military or para-military, of either Party into any part of the Demilitarized Zone, when confirmed by the United Nations representatives referred to in the following sub-paragraph, shall constitute a flagrant violation of this Agreement.'

Extract from the 1949 Israeli-Syrian General Armistice Agreement

Many generals in the Israeli Defence Force wanted a war simply because they believed they would win. They were concerned by the threat posed by Syria, which had been armed by the USSR. They deliberately provoked the Syrians on the border in the Golan Heights. In April 1967, the Syrians, as expected, responded by firing in a demilitarized zone. This gave the Israelis an excuse to shoot down six Syrian fighter planes over Syria and Israeli pilots added insult to injury by flying a victory lap over Damascus, the Syrian capital. This incident helped Israeli generals build the case that war with Syria and Egypt was inevitable and winnable.

'In June 1967 we again had a choice. The Egyptian army concentrations in the Sinai approaches do not prove that Nasser was really about to attack us. We must be honest with ourselves. We decided to attack him. This was a war of self-defence in the noblest sense of the term. The government of national unity then established decided unanimously: We will take the initiative and attack the enemy, drive him back, and thus assure the security of Israel and the future of the nation.

We did not do this for lack of an alternative. We could have gone on waiting. We could have sent the army home. Who knows if there would have been an attack against us? There is no proof of it. There are several arguments to the contrary. While it is indeed true that the closing of the Straits of Tiran was an act of aggression, a causus belli, there is always room for a great deal of consideration as to whether it is necessary to make a causus into a bellum.'

Address by Menachem Begin, Prime Minister of Israel, at the National Defence College, 8 August 1982

'Never mind that. After all, I know how at least 80 percent of the clashes there started. In my opinion, more than 80 percent, but let's talk about 80 percent. It went this way: We would send a tractor to plow someplace where it wasn't possible to do anything, in the demilitarized area, and knew in advance that the Syrians would start to shoot. If they didn't shoot, we would tell the tractor to advance farther, until in the end the Syrians would get annoyed and shoot. And then we would use artillery and later the air force also, and that's how it was. I did that, and Laskov and Chara [Zvi Tsur, Rabin's predecessor as chief of staff] did that, and Yitzhak did that, but it seems to me that the person who most enjoyed these games was Dado [David Elazar, OC Northern Command, 1964– 69].'

Moshe Dayan, Israeli Defence Minister in 1967

In 1966, Israel's remarkable economic growth through the 1950s and 1960s went into reverse as a recession hit and unemployment soared. The threat of Arab aggression and terrorism attacks inside Israel turned this economic crisis into a more general crisis about Israel's security as a state. The government tried to avoid war but through the spring and early summer an increasingly fearful public put them under enormous pressure. The new state, grasped so eagerly by its founders in the shadow of the Holocaust, was still less than twenty years old. Something had to be done to show Israel could stand firm and defend itself.

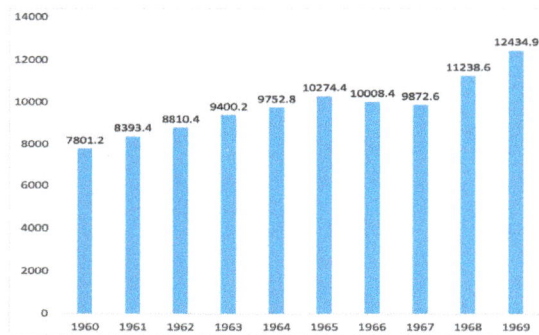

Israel's GDP per capita per year in US Dollars. Source: The World Bank

'[1966] was marked with economic recession and social distress. The prospect of a third war in two decades was yet another source of melancholy. Many felt that the very existence of the state was at stake. Dark humor was a source of comic relief, and comments like "The last one to leave the airport should turn off the lights" became widespread. Indeed, many did leave the country, exacerbating concerns that the young state might well be no more than a fleeting chapter in history.

Prime Minister Levi Eshkol also served as minister of defense, despite his lack of military background. This only caused further damage to his shaky public image. Army officers pressed him to make a decision and essentially forced him to appoint the legendary General Moshe Dayan in his place as minister of defense just days before the onset of the war.

The ambience reeked of lack of vision, a collective sense of a lost way, nurturing sentiments of national depression and uncertainty.'

Extract from Sarah Ozacky-Lazar. 'The Seven Good Years? Israel, 1967 - 1973: The Critical Change.' Israel Studies 23, no.3 (2018), p.18

After years of rapid economic growth in the 1950s and early 1960s, it was a shock to Israelis when a recession hit in 1966. Israelis blamed the government for economic mismanagement and the government nearly fell. Israel's political leaders knew that the army and air-force were well-prepared and calculated that a good war would rally the country and distract attention from the economy. So, the government not only exaggerated the external threat to Israel from its Arab neighbours, but also provoked conflict. The Israeli government's strategy worked because the Israeli public and press were willing to embrace war as an answer to their other problems.

The Shalom Meir Tower in Tel Aviv opened in 1965. It was the tallest building in the Middle East at the time

'The problems are many: economic recession with attendant unemployment; religious controversy between Orthodox and secular Jews over such questions as the performance of autopsies and the use of vehicular transport on the Sabbath; 'racial' differences between the early immigrants from Europe and the later influx of illiterate and impoverished Jews from North Africa and Asia, and a political split between the moderate, and elderly, leaders who have long governed the semi-theocratic state and the young, native-born sabras [Jews born in Israel] who urge a stronger, more vigorous policy toward the Arabs. For a time at least, the June call to arms and subsequent victory salved these divisions in the national fabric.'

From 'Blossoming Socialism to Successful Capitalism' by Sever Plotzker, 'Economic' supplement Independence Day, Yediot Achronot newspaper 23 April 2007, pp.2-3

71

Egypt's President Gamal Abdel Nasser tipped Israel over the edge and triggered the war. On 13th May, the USSR provided a false intelligence report to Cairo saying Israel was about to attack Egypt's ally, Syria. Nasser assembled his army on the border with Israel three days later and expelled the UN peacekeeping force stationed there. Then, on 22nd May, he closed the Straits of Tiran to Israeli shipping. The Israeli government reminded Cairo that back in 1957 it stated it would interpret the closure of the Straits of Tiran as an act of war. When Nasser refused to negotiate, Israel had no choice but to take military action and so it attacked the Egyptian air-forces on 5th June 1967.

'[Nasser] could not afford to remain inactive, because his leadership of the Arab world was being challenged. Since the Samu raid the Jordanians had been accusing him of cowardice and of hiding from the Israelis behind the skirts of the UN Emergency Force in Sinai. Syria had a defense pact with Egypt that compelled it to go to Syria's aid in the event of an Israeli attack. Clearly, Nasser had to do something, both to preserve his own credibility as an ally and to restrain the hotheads in Damascus. There is general agreement among commentators that Nasser neither wanted nor planned to go to war with Israel. What he did was to embark on an exercise in brinkmanship that was to carry him over the brink.

Nasser took three steps that were intended to impress Arab public opinion rather than be a conscious prelude to war with Israel. The first step was to send a large number of troops into Sinai. The second was to ask for the removal of the UN Emergency Force from Sinai. The third and most fateful step, taken on 22 May, was to close the Straits of Tiran to Israeli shipping. For Israel this constituted a casus belli...Nasser understood the psychological significance of this step...In closing the Straits of Tiran to Israeli shipping, he took a terrible gamble—and lost.'

Extract from 'The Iron Wall: Israel and the Arab World' (2001) by Avi Shlaim, p.237

Cartoon from Lebanese newspaper Al-Farida shows Nasser kicking a Jew into the sea, with the armies of Lebanon, Syria and Iraq supporting him

Both the USA and the USSR pursued policies that made war in the Middle East more likely. The USSR sent false intelligence reports to Egypt in May 1967 warning that Israel was about to attack Syria. Egypt had a mutual defence pact with Syria, so Nasser had no choice but to deploy the Egyptian army on the Israeli border. It is still not clear why the USSR did this. Meanwhile, US President Lyndon Johnson, who could have corrected the false USSR report, chose not to. It suited the USA to see Egypt weakened because it was an ally of the Soviets in the Middle East. His policy was in sharp contrast with President Eisenhower's 10 years earlier; in 1955 the US had stopped Israel from invading Egypt to help out the British at Suez.

'Brezhnev's report shows that Moscow had no intention of inciting an armed conflict in the Middle East and that the June 1967 war was the result of grave miscalculations and of Soviet inability to control the Arabs, rather than a conspiracy. The brief documents that throughout April-May, 1967, the Kremlin suspected that Israel was planning an act of aggression against Syria. Determined to forestall the Israeli offensive and to rescue the new radical-left regime in Damascus, the Soviet government informed Egypt that Israel had mobilized its armed forces on the border with Syria. By doing so, Moscow hoped to manipulate Nasser into assisting Syria by concentrating his armed forces on Egypt's border with Israel. The Kremlin estimated mistakenly, as if turned out, that Israel was militarily weak and could not cope with a war on two fronts. Subsequently, Moscow consented to the ejection of United Nations (UN) peacekeeping forces from outposts on the Israeli-Egyptian border, and to the concentration of Egyptian troops on the Sinai Peninsula and the Gaza Strip.'

'The Soviet Union and the Six-Day War: Revelations from the Polish Archives, July 27, 2011', by Uri Bar-Noi, CWIHP e-Dossier No.8

Washington, June 1, 1967.

Conversation between Major General Meir Amit and Secretary McNamara – late afternoon, 1 June 1967

...Gen. Amit then went on to describe the situation as he sees it which is to the effect that the blockade of Tiran is window dressing. He believes a grand design, which he termed the "Domino Effect," has now developed. That is, that the UAR, with Russian backing, hopes to roll up the whole of the Middle East all the way to the borders of Russia, to include Iran, under Arab domination. While this whole matter is close to and vital for Israel, the long range effect would be deeply inimical to U.S. interests....

Gen. Amit, returning to his main theme, stressed his opinion that it is a U.S. problem as much as an Israeli problem, and maybe even more so, and that he feels extreme measures are needed quickly...

In closing the meeting Mr. McNamara thanked Gen. Amit for his candid discussion and indicated that he, the Secretary, would be seeing the President shortly and would convey Amit's views to him...

Rufus Taylor
Vice Admiral, U.S. Navy
Deputy Director of Central Intelligence

'Foreign Relations of the United States, 1964-68'. Volume XIX, Arab-Israeli Crisis and War 1967

CHAPTER 6

The First Intifada 1987-1993

Was Israel's response to Palestinian unrest unnecessarily violent?

In the aftermath of the Six Days' War, Jordan withdrew from the West Bank and Egypt withdrew from the Gaza Strip. This left Israel responsible for maintaining law and order and providing stability for the Palestinian population in those areas. Israel's security forces were stretched in the 1980s. It had been forced to invade Lebanon in 1982 to prevent guerrilla attacks, and by 1985 was having to maintain a permanent occupation and buffer zone in South Lebanon. In this context, an uprising in the West Bank was an unwelcome distraction for military authorities and an expense for the government which had to call up army reservists to cope with security demands. Not surprisingly the Israeli authorities wanted to nip the protests in the bud.

'The first immediate trigger was the 26 November hang glider incident, in which a young Palestinian guerilla entered Israel and succeeded in killing 6 Israeli soldiers.'

Extract from 'The Uprising: Causes and Consequences' by Gail Pressberg, Journal of Palestine Studies, 1988

Palestinian barricades during the First Intifada

Israel had used their surprise attack in 1967 to achieve their long term territorial ambitions. They had seized the whole of the West Bank and Gaza plus East Jerusalem, the site of the Old City and the al-Aqsa Mosque – over the next twenty years they secured their control over the Palestinians by building forts and Jewish settlements, and forcing Palestinians off their land. Palestinians were governed under military law which tolerated no dissent or opposition. In an overwhelming majority, this military occupation had been declared illegal by the United Nations. Palestinians were entitled to protest an inhumane military occupation and subsequent infringements of their rights.

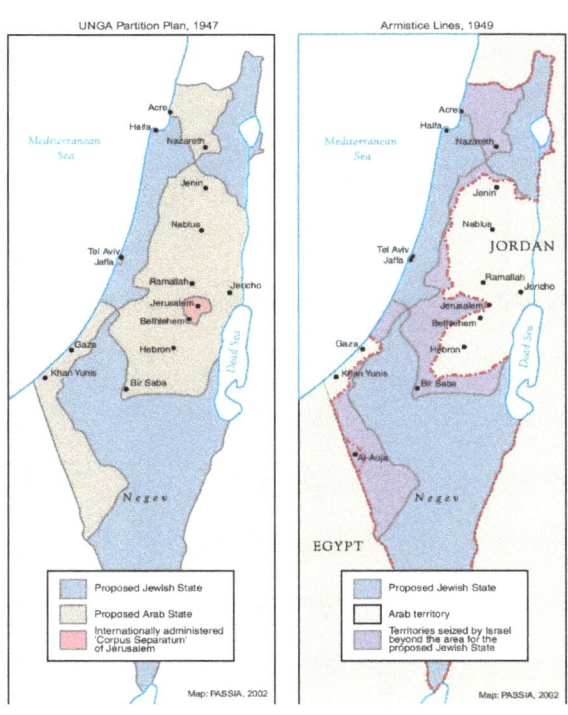

Map comparing the UN-proposed Israeli State to the land seized by Israel

Swedish peacekeepers are forced to flee from Hill 88 near Gaza due to Israeli strikes on the area in 1967

77

The protest movement in the West Bank described itself as part of civil society but this was not accurate. In fact, the trigger for the unrest was a false rumour about a traffic accident. This rumour was compounded by completely false allegations that IDF soldiers had poisoned villagers' wells. The thinly spread IDF soldiers, many of them with very little combat experience and no riot equipment like shields or helmets were very vulnerable to stone throwing. When they sheltered inside armoured cars the rioters started to throw Molotov cocktails – there were over three thousand petrol bomb attacks during the first four years of the Intifada.

On the Destruction of Israel:

'Israel will exist and will continue to exist until Islam will obliterate it, just as it obliterated others before it.' (Preamble)

The Exclusive Muslim Nature of the Area:
"The land of Palestine is an Islamic Waqf consecrated for future Moslem generations until Judgement Day. It, or any part of it, should not be squandered: it, or any part of it, should not be given up.' (Article 11)

'Liberation of Palestine is then an individual duty for every Moslem.' (Article 14)

Extract from the Covenant of Hamas, 1988

'After the 1979 revolution, Iran ended its alliance with Israel and started supporting the Palestinians, symbolized by turning over the Israeli embassy in Tehran to the Palestine Liberation Organization.

As part of its campaign to export the revolution, the theocracy also aided emerging Palestinian Islamic groups, notably Islamic Jihad and Hamas. Both sent representatives to Tehran.'

Extract from 'The Iran Primer: Power, Politics and US Policy', R. Brandenburg, 2010

Photos and news footage of the Intifada show how the protests emerged from the streets, and evolved in the face of Israeli violence. After the initial peaceful marches were violently broken up, protesters used graffiti, shop boycotts and eventually picked up stones. Palestinians sometimes call the First Intifada 'the Stone Intifada'. There are hundreds of photos of young boys throwing stones at tanks. And for the first time much of the leadership of the protest movement was led by women. The IDF claimed the protests were coordinated by terrorist groups, but this was false. The IDF had the only hammer in the room and as a consequence wanted to define every problem it saw as a nail.

Palestinian woman protests the actions of IDF soldiers in 1987

IDF soldier requesting a resident of Jabalia to erase a slogan on a wall during the First Intifada, February 1988

Israel was responding to an attack that was unjustified; many of the problems and grievances held by Palestinians against Israel were rooted in problems caused by their own weak leadership, or the policies of neighbouring Arab nations which contributed to instability in the region. The PLO, and the whole of the Palestinian leadership under Yasser Arafat, first unwelcome in Jordan and later expelled from Beirut in Lebanon, were now thousands of miles away in Tunisia. They were out of touch with the problems of the Palestinian people. Consequently, many Palestinians felt angry and abandoned and blamed Israel. And when Jordan and Egypt governed the West Bank and Gaza respectively, they had done very little to improve the economic or political conditions of the Palestinians.

President Jimmy Carter shaking hands with Egyptian President Anwar Sadat and Israeli Prime Minister Menachem Begin at the signing of the Egyptian-Israeli Peace Treaty in the grounds of the White House, 26 March 1979

'Recognition of this fact led Jordan and the PLO to cooperate despite frosty relations...[they were] driven closer by President Sadat's political initiative of 1977 and the subsequent peace negotiations between Egypt and Israel...[the PLO] felt obliged to move into a common 'steadfastness' with the more radical Arab states.'

Extract about the frustrations felt by Palestinians after Israel and Egypt signed a peace treaty, effectively bringing the role of Egypt in the Palestinian cause to an end. From 'Palestine and Israel: The Uprising and Beyond', D. McDowell, 1989

In the twenty years after their victory Israeli leaders refused to make any arrangements for the governance of the millions of Palestinians they controlled. To do so would force them to either give back the land, as ordered by the UN, or annex it permanently and so confirm their intention to keep the Palestinians as permanent second-class citizens. This was not something the US could publicly allow. So, the Palestinians were left with no self-government, no opportunities for political expression and no outlet for political protest apart from on the street. Palestinian leaders had been forced into exile in Tunis and even there they were not safe. In 1988 a key Palestinian figure, Khalil al-Wazir, was assassinated by Israeli commandos.

6. It is forbidden to print or publicize in the region any publication of notice, poster, photo, pamphlet or other document containing material having a political significance, unless a license is previously obtained from the military commander of the place in which it is intended to exercise the printing or publication.

7. Any person who –

   A. attempts, orally or in another manner, to influence public opinion in the region in a manner that is liable to harm public safety or public order, or

   B. does any act or has in his possession any object with the intent to do or facilitate the commission of an attempt as aforesaid,

will be charged with violating this Order.

Extract of IDF Order 101 restricting the freedom of expression for Palestinians

The 1967 War was over
All the land of Palestine was occupied
In every patch of land there was a tragedy
In every house a sad old man
In every village there was poverty
And in every camp an orphaned child!
They reckoned the case was over
And thought they had gotten rid of us
Once and for all!
They thought that after all the suffering
We had lost our patience
Or given up our steadfastness
A million times did we tell them:
No to Camp David
A million NOs to it and to all those behind it
No to autonomy: it is futile and deformed!
No to elections. They take our rights away
They replace our rules
And divide us more and more
Our demand is one:
An independent state
That only will last forever.

Extract from a Palestinian Folk Poem

The Palestinians claimed that they had got worse off since 1967 and the arrival of Israeli forces, but the reality was different. In fact, it was in Israel's interest to have a prosperous, well-educated Palestinian population. Roughly one million Palestinians in the Israeli occupied territories had benefitted from improved access to education, electricity, and infrastructure after 1967. This was thanks to the Israeli ethos of 'enlightened occupation'. GDP in the West Bank had grown alongside Israel's and unemployment rates had fallen. Had Israel lost control, Palestinians would have been very much worse off. The Israeli reaction to the Intifada may have looked tough on TV, but the alternative of lawlessness would have been much worse for the Palestinians.

Box 2.1 Occupied Territories—Key Socioeconomic Indicators

	1970	1980
Population (000)	980	1,181
GNP per capita (1991 US$)	780	1,700
GDP per capita (1991 US$)	670	1,310
Wage income from Israel (% of GNP)	12	24
Share of industry (% of GDP)	5	7
Exports (% of GNP)	22	23
Imports (% of GNP)	47	46
Employment (000s) in OT	160	141
Employment (000s) in Israel	21	75
Primary enrollment (000s)	179	259
Secondary enrollment (000s)	26	53
Hospital beds (per 1,000 pop.)	—	1.9
Birth rate (per 1,000 pop.)	42	48
Daily per capita calorie consumption	2,300	2,650
Life expectancy (years)	56	61
Infant mortality (per 1,000 live births)	95	65
Households with electricity (%)	30	66
Households with safe water (%)	15	47
Households with refrigerators (%)	11	57
Households with washing machines (%)	—	23
Households with automobiles (%)	2	—

Sources: Statistical Abstracts of Israel, Central Bureau of Statistics, various issues. Mission estima

Table showing economic growth in the Occupied Territories in 1970-1980

MYTH
"Israel closed West Bank schools during the intifada to deprive Palestinians of an education."

FACT
Educational opportunities in the territories greatly improved under Israeli rule. The number of elementary and secondary schools increased by more than a third from 1967-88. Women were major beneficiaries of the boom. From 1970-86, for example, the percentage of women who had not attended school was slashed by more than half, from 67 percent to 32 percent. Before 1967, no universities existed on the West Bank; six were built under Israel's administration.
Despite the intifada, nursery schools, kindergartens and most West Bank vocational schools remained open because none were used to instigate violence. Gaza schools also stayed open because militant Islamic fundamentalists there used the mosques, not schools, to incite their followers.
The PLO used many schools, however, to stimulate attacks against Israelis. Caches of knives, clubs and iron bars were found hidden in school buildings. "Schools are the natural place for a demonstration to begin," wrote Palestinian journalist Daoud Kuttab. "In school, demonstrations and stone-throwing are part of a tradition....To hit an Israeli car is to become a hero."
In 1988, Israel closed some secondary schools and colleges in the West Bank that were being used to orchestrate the insurrection. After it announced the closures, Israel offered to reopen any school whose principal would guarantee that his school would be used to educate children, not to encourage rioting. But educators, many cowed by the uprising leadership, remained silent. When the violence subsided, Israel reopened all high schools, colleges and universities.

Entry in the Jewish Virtual Library on education and school closures in the West Bank during the First Intifada

The illegal Israeli occupation caused economic difficulties for Palestinians. The Israeli government deliberately weakened indigenous Palestinian industries like soap manufacture from oil and made much of the Palestinian labour force dependent on Israeli based employment. When the Israeli economy entered a downturn, it was the Palestinian Arab workers who lost their jobs in Israel first. Israeli economic policies were designed to protect Israeli industry and Israeli settlers. Capital investment and infrastructure investment was minimal in the West Bank or Gaza, whereas settlements were liberally supplied with new roads, power supplies and water. Palestinians had a right to protest these conditions.

'There will be no development in the occupied territories instigated by the Israeli government, and no permits will be given for expanding agriculture or industry, which may compete with the State of Israel.'

Former and future Israeli Prime Minister Yitzhak Rabin in the Jerusalem Post, 15 February 1985

'Phase III-early 1980s until Intifada in 1987. This phase is characterized by stagnation and declining employment opportunities. The collapse of the regional oil boom prompted a decline in worker remittances from the Gulf. While continued growth in Israel provided a cushion from the regional slowdown, employment in Israel was virtually flat in the mid-1980s. Beginning with the Intifada, employment for Palestinians in manufacturing and services declined. This decline was offset by a rise in construction employment in response to an Israeli housing boom, resulting from a surge in immigration. However, recession and near hyperinflation in Israel had a serious impact on the 35 percent of the Palestinian labor force employed in Israel, and on the majority of Palestinian trade with Israel. Once work opportunities abroad declined, there was increased pressure to employ workers at home.'

Extract from 'Development Under Adversity: The Palestinian Economy in Transition', edited by Ishac Diwan and Radwan A. Shaban, Palestine Economic Policy Research Institute (MAS) and the World Bank', March 1995

Israel's intervention eventually proved successful. The uprising became less popular as the PLO came back from exile and attempted to take control of the protest movement and steer it in an even more radical direction. Many Palestinians withdrew support for the Intifada, recognizing that peaceful engagement with the Israeli authorities would achieve more than force. Radical Palestinians accused moderates of collaboration with Israel and used that as an excuse to execute anyone who disagreed with them. Israel was acting in the interest of the majority, by bringing the violence to a swift end and minimise casualties.

'This report deals with the responsibility of Palestinian political organizations and their activists for the torture and killing of Palestinians suspected of collaborating with the Israeli authorities during the Intifada... According to the Israel Defense Forces (IDF) Spokesperson, 942 Palestinians were killed by other Palestinians on suspicion of collaboration between December 9, 1987, when the Intifada erupted, and November 30, 1993.1 The Associated Press puts the number at 771.'

Extract from the Summary of B'Tselem report: 'Collaborators in the Occupied Territories: Human Rights Abuses and Violations', January 1994

'[T]he Intifada seemed to have lost direction. A symptom of the PLO's frustration was the great increase in the killing of suspected collaborators." Roughly 18,000 Palestinians, compromised by Israeli intelligence, are said to have given information to the other side.'

Extract from 'Righteous Victims: a History of the Zionist-Arab conflict, 1881–1999', by Benny Morris, 1999

Despite its succession of military victories since 1948, Israel had managed to maintain an image of itself as a Jewish David against an Arab Goliath. The stone throwing boys of the First Intifada were never going to defeat the strongest army in the Middle East, but they did break this image. Israelis continued to regard themselves as the perennial victim, but for many in the international community, their cruelty and arrogance was now on show. TV news viewers were shocked that Prime Minister Rabin had ordered his soldiers to break the arms and legs of demonstrators. The First Intifada established a pattern now repeated many times since. When Israeli forces met Palestinian opposition of any kind the escalation from non-lethal to lethal forces was almost instant.

Palestinians killed in the Occupied Territories (including East Jerusalem)

Year	Palestinians killed by Israeli security forces	Of them: Minors under age 17	Palestinians killed by Israeli civilians	Of them: Minors under age 17
Dec 9-31 1987	22	5	0	0
1988	289	48	15	2
1989	285	78	17	5
1990	125	23	9	2
1991	91	24	6	3
1992	134	23	2	0
1993-13.9.93	124	36	5	1
14.9.93-31.12.93	30	4	8	0
1994	106	16	38	8
1995	42	4	2	1
1996	69	10	3	1
1997	18	5	4	0
1998	21	3	6	0
1999	8	0	0	0
2000 until 28.9	12	2	0	0
Total	1,376	281	115	23

Israelis killed in the Occupied Territories (including East Jerusalem)

Year	Israeli civilians killed by Palestinians	Of them: Minors under age 17	Israeli security forces personnel killed by Palestinians
Dec 9-31 1987	0	0	0
1988	6	3	4
1989	3	0	6
1990	4	0	3
1991	7	0	1
1992	11	0	14
1993-13.9.93	16	0	15
14.9.93-31.12.93	11	0	3
1994	11	0	12
1995	7	0	9
1996	3	1	19
1997	4	0	0
1998	8	0	3
1999	1	0	2
2000 until 28.9	2	0	0
Total	94	4	91

Casualty figures for the First Intifada

Resolution 607

Territories occupied by Israel

Abstract

Resolution 607 (1988) of 5 January 1988

The Security Council,

Recalling its resolution 605 (1987) of 22 December 1987,

Expressing grave concern over the situation in the occupied Palestinian territories,

Having been apprised of the decision of Israel, the occupying Power, to "continue the deportation" of Palestinian civilians in the occupied territories,

Recalling the Geneva Convention relative to the Protection of Civilian Persons in Time of War, of 12 August 1949, and in particular articles 47 and 49 of same,

1. Reaffirms once again that the Geneva Convention relative to the Protection of Civilian Persons in Time of War, of 12 August 1949, is applicable to Palestinians and other Arab territories occupied by Israel since 1967, including Jerusalem;

2. Calls upon Israel to refrain from deporting any Palestinian civilians from the occupied territories;

3. Strongly requests Israel, the occupying Power, to abide by its obligations arising from the Convention;

4. Decides to keep the situation in the Palestinian and other Arab territories occupied by Israel since 1967, including Jerusalem, under review.

UN Security Council Resolution 607, issued in 1988 to address violations of previous UN resolutions and Geneva Code laws

CHAPTER 7

The failure of the Peace Process after 1993

Who has been more to blame for the failure of the 'Peace Process?'

The Palestinians are to blame for the failure of the Peace Process. They have failed to accept their own defeats. They have failed to show that they can live as peaceful neighbours. It is seventy-five years since their defeat in 1948. In 1993 the Palestinian leader Yasser Arafat, under intense American pressure, wrote to Israeli PM Yitzhak Shamir saying the PLO recognized Israel's right to exist. Yet, many continue to see Israel as only existing temporarily. The Hamas Charter states that Hamas 'rejects any alternative to the full and complete liberation of Palestine, from the river to the sea.' The Palestinian insistence on clinging onto the notion of 'steadfastness' is a roadblock to tangible peace outcomes. Such unrealistic and rigid expectations of outcomes simply prevent any headway being made in the peace process. For example, Palestinians still refuse to accept the permanent loss of former homes – a potent symbol of that is the key symbol on the entrance of refugee camps. And the reason there are Palestinians housed in camps, after so many decades, is that Palestinian governments and neighbouring Arab governments have refused to give those refugees citizenship.

Photograph of the Shatila refugee camp, Beirut, Lebanon, 22 June 2006

'The Palestinians were surely betrayed in the past, and they surely have suffered [...] But they have also helped to ensure their status as victims. Never seizing opportunities when they presented themselves. Blaming others for their predicament. Declaring unmistakable defeats as victories.'

Dennis Ross, the US Chief negotiator in 2000, reflecting on the Palestinian leader, Yasser Arafat's failure to accept Israeli peace terms

Israelis are to blame for the failure of the Peace Process. They have failed to recognise the Palestinians' right to self-determination and to a state. The Palestinians were persuaded by the Americans under the Oslo Agreements in the mid 1990s to give up their claim to 78% of historic Palestine in return for a state of their own on the remaining 22%. But instead of embracing this extraordinarily generous offer, Israelis immediately set about sabotaging the deal. Their strategy has been simple but relentless – every single Israeli government since 1967 has expanded illegal settlements on the lands designated for a Palestinian state. In the mid 90s there were 250,000 illegal settlers and by 2024 there were over 700,000. Those illegal communities are connected by separate roads, have their own water and power supplies, even their own universities which have been built and funded by Israel. An arial view of Israeli development over the West Bank reveals a clear pattern in which Palestinian population centres are separated by bands of Israeli infrastructure.

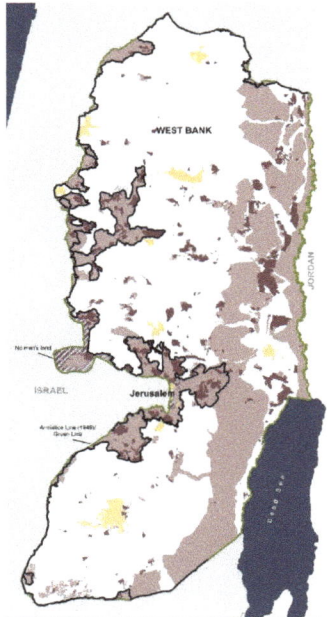

Map of Israeli settlements in the West Bank and East Jerusalem, January 2006. The areas in white show the areas which were not affected by Israeli infrastructure/settlements/military outposts. The areas in yellow are Palestinian urban centres.

'Israeli settlements in the Occupied Palestinian territories have expanded by a record amount and risk eliminating any practical possibly of a Palestinian state [...] the growth of Israeli settlements amounted to the transfer by Israel of its own population which is a war crime [...] Settler violence and settlement-related violations have reached shocking new levels, and risk eliminating any practical possibility of establishing a viable Palestinian State.'

The United Nations High Commissioner for Human Rights Volker Turk in statement in Geneva March 8, 2024

Without a legitimate Palestinian body to negotiate with, it is impossible for Israel to pursue peace. The successor to Yasser Arafat, Mahmoud Abbas, lacks the authority to maintain a united front amongst Palestinians. Abbas also lacks democratic legitimacy since no elections have been held since 2006. Corruption, cronyism and incompetence have eroded the reputation of the Palestinian Authority, which controls services along the West Bank. This problem of having no Palestinian partner for peace with whom to negotiate was greatly exacerbated in 2007, when Hamas, a radical Islamic party, seized control of the government of Gaza in a bloody coup. Since then, there have been two Palestinian governments, one of which is a terror organization intent on murdering Israelis.

'Today a staggering 87% of Palestinians in the West Bank and Gaza believe that the PA is corrupt, 78% want Abbas to resign and 62% believe that the PA is a liability. This loss of popular legitimacy has had real life implications even before the current war in Gaza, areas of the West Bank were practically ungoverned. The international community, appalled by the PA's corruption and dealing with competing crises elsewhere, reduced aid. Diplomatically outside powers continued to treat the PA as the legitimate representative of the Palestinians. But in reality, world leaders have largely given up on it.'

Extract from an article published by the Washington Institute for Near East Policy by Ghaith al-Omari, October 19, 2023

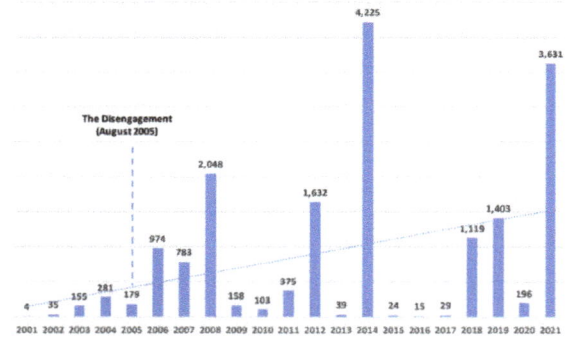

Number of rockets fired at Israel from the Gaza Strip by year

90

The Israelis have never offered themselves as a reasonable partner at the negotiating table because they have never been open to any reasonable peace deal. Israeli Jews make up about 50% of the population living between the Mediterranean and the River Jordan; the other 50% are Arab Palestinians, (and this count excludes Palestinian exiles living in Jordan, Syria, and Lebanon). Every peace deal offered to the Jews has always favoured them in terms of giving them more land than their population justifies and yet they always cry 'unfair'. The Oslo Accords were a very generous deal for Israel and the offer was made by Arafat, the one Palestinian leader in a generation strong enough to have delivered it. Indeed, it was not an extremist Arab Palestinian who shot Arafat dead as punishment for surrendering Muslim lands, it was an extremist Israeli Jew who shot Rabin dead as punishment for surrendering Jewish lands.

'The fact is that Israel has conceded nothing, as former Secretary Of State James Baker said in a TV interview, except, blandly, the existence of "the PLO as the representative of the Palestinian people". Or as the Israeli "dove" Amos Oz reportedly put it in the course of a BBC interview, "this is the second biggest victory in the history of Zionism."'

Edward Said, Palestinian intellectual, in the London Review of Books, 21 October 1993

'Yitzhak Rabin was murdered in a political assassination. He was murdered in a political assassination with the cooperation of Benjamin Netanyahu and [Itamar] Ben Gvir,'

Merav Michaeli, chief of the Labor party in Israel speaking on the 27th anniversary of Rabin's death, October 24, 2022

The Middle East attracts enormous outside interference and most of it is neither well-intentioned towards Israel nor helping Palestinians get to a peace settlement. The USSR support for the PLO prevented peace in the 1970s as did Iran's supply of missiles to Gaza in the 2010s. The Gulf States have financed massive mosque building for Palestinians which has radicalised Palestinian youth. Supposed allies lobbied Israel to stop it taking more decisive measures to permanently settle the Palestinian problem, and in doing so exercising a double standard that appears antisemitic. It did not escape Israeli attention that western powers who in the past routinely moved hundreds of thousands of subject peoples around without their consent, were outraged when Israeli authorities want to move a family out of their house.

Hamas leader, Ismail Haniyeh, meets Iranian Ayatollah Ali Khamenei, 22 June 2023

Russian President Vladimir Putin greets Yasser Arafat, 11 August 2000

The end of the Cold War and fall of the USSR left Palestine without any protector, and Israel benefiting from its close alliance with the USA, the remaining superpower. This has been an obstacle to peace because it has given Israel the sense that it is untouchable and will have to make no compromises. The USA's efforts to make peace in the 1990s lacked balance and US politicians were easily outmanoeuvred by their more strategic Israeli colleagues. The Trump peace plan of 2020 entitled 'Peace to Prosperity: A Vision to Improve the Lives of the Palestinian and Israeli People' has been even more obviously and quickly unsuccessful in its aim. International support in the form of multi-decade funding for the UN institutions that run much of civil governance for Palestinians, while necessary each year, has over the long term become harmful. By insulating the Israelis from the true cost of their occupation, it perpetuates it.

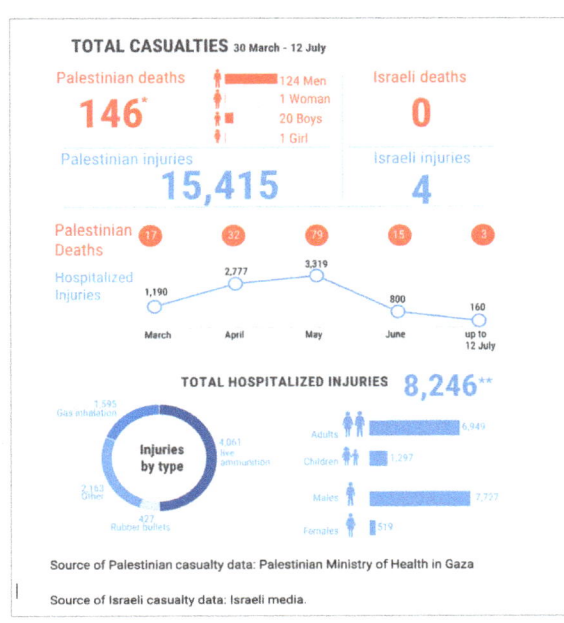

On May 14, 2018, the US opened an embassy in Jerusalem against Palestinian wishes. That day Israeli forces killed over 58 Palestinians on the Gaza border protesting the US move.

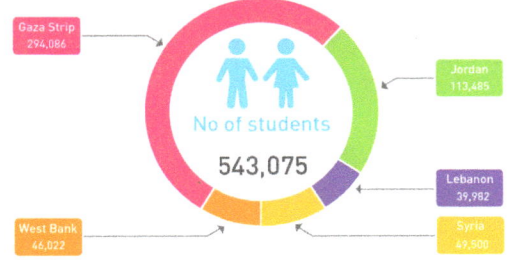

Number of Palestinian refugee students enrolled in 2024 in schools operated by the United Nations Relief and Works Agency for Palestine refugees in the near east

Israel was successful in making peace with its immediate neighbours, Egypt in 1979, and Jordan in 1994, and in this context the Oslo deal with the Palestinians looked possible. However, Palestinian terrorism during the Second Intifada showed the Oslo Accords were not leading to sustainable progress towards peace. Since then, terrorist attacks have continued, along with rocket attacks from Hamas in Gaza against Israel. Conflict and instability across the Middle East have further undermined the prospects of peace negotiations. In the last few years Israel has achieved much improved relations with the Gulf States and, to some extent, with Saudia Arabia based on trade and investment. For the sake of Arab audiences at home, Gulf leaders bring up the position of the Palestinians and especially the question of religious access to al-Aqsa Mosque for Muslim worshippers. However, in spite of efforts it has been hard to make any substantive progress on, for example, rights of religious access, the status of East Jerusalem, control of the Jordan Valley, the Palestinian right of return or the removal of unauthorised settlements in the West Bank.

King Hussein of Jordan lights Israeli Prime Minister, Yizhak Rabin's cigarette at Aqaba, Jordan, 26 October 1994, after signing the peace treaty

Israeli Prime Minister Netanyahu and the Foreign Ministers from UAE and Bahrain sign the Abraham Accords with US President Trump at the White House, 15 September 2020.

Within months of President Rabin's assassination in 1995 by a gunman who claimed that he acted with religious authority, Israeli politics tilted towards religious nationalism under the leadership of Benjamin Netanyahu. A combination of immigration from the former Soviet Union and a high birth rate amongst Ultra-Orthodox Jews, has pushed the Israeli population towards religious nationalism. Younger Israelis are much less likely to agree to swap land for peace than their elders. Without a democratic mandate to make peace with the Palestinians, no Israeli government has made any serious attempt to revive discussions. They have all been content with the status quo. PM Netanyahu has been leading an increasingly right-wing government which is more interested in seizing control of the Israeli state by neutering the Supreme Court and the independent press. Leading members of this government openly encourage the ethnic cleansing of Palestinians in East Jerusalem and the West Bank, and genocide against Gazans. Peace is the last thing on their minds.

'Russian immigrants are criticised for bringing with them right wing sentiments that have fuelled the rise of parties espousing pro-settler, xenophobic and anti-democratic agendas that have overpowered Israel's left and complicated peace prospects with the Palestinians. Bill Clinton [...] once lumped them together with settlers as the "hardest core people against the division of the land" with the Palestinians. Ghassan Khatib, the spokesman for the Palestinian Authority described them as a boon to "aggressive and colonialist tendencies in Israel, and their immigration has helped shift Israel to the right - to the disadvantage of peace possibilities.'

Hugh Naylor 'Russian Immigrants Have Pushed Israel to the Right' The National News June 24, 2012

'In the words of another former prime minister, Ehud Barak, Netanyahu, who himself faces corruption charges, is "determined to degrade Israel into a corrupt and racist dictatorship that will crumble society". The situation in Israel is unique, of course. None the less many have observed a slide from "democracy to autarchy" under Netanyahu similar to that in other countries with autocratically inclined leaders such as Modi in India, Erdogan in Turkey, and Orban in Hungary. According to the American Brookings Institution: "Each of these leaders has made similar efforts to co-opt judicial institutions and exploit or change the rules of the game for their own private advantage, which have catalysed their country's degeneration from a democracy to an authoritarian or mixed regime.'

Adam Boulton 'Netanyahu's Power Grab is Tearing Society Apart and Delighting Israel's Enemies' Sky News July 30, 2023

Israelis, for long term historical reasons, place a high premium on security and any peace deal must take this into account. Israel and Israelis have been the subject of attack by Palestinians and their supporters since the state of Israel was founded in 1948. Each decade these attacks take a different form – cross border raids in the 1950s and 60s, terror bombings and hijacks across every decade from the 60s to the 2020s and rocket attacks from Gaza from 2002 right up to now. The October 7th 2023 attack was by far the worst suffered but it should be seen in the context of a very long running cycle of violence sponsored by Palestinians, and not as an aberration. But the lesson of October 7th for Israelis was that they need to maintain even stricter control on Palestinians in the future.

The aftermath of a Palestinian suicide bomb attack on a bus in Tel Aviv, Israel, which killed five people, 24 July 1995

Detail from a 14th century Spanish church altarpiece showing Jews profaning Christian symbols

Palestinians too would like to have a modicum of security and freedom of movement. A peace deal must take this into account. Western media and politicians refer to the Israeli Palestinian 'conflict' which is a fundamental misnomer. Here one wealthy state (Israel), protected by a first world army with nuclear weapons, supported by a world superpower (the USA), oppress a poorer, weaker group of stateless people. Israel controls all of the borders of the West Bank and Gaza, they have built army forts, outposts and settlements across the West Bank, a security barrier dividing the West Bank, they've taken away Palestinian airports and ports, they have an extensive system of informers, listening devices, and surveillance. They collect Palestinian taxes and choose when to hand them over, and statistics gathered by the UN show that Israelis kill twenty times more Palestinians than Palestinians kill Israelis. It's not a conflict. It's an oppression.

Israeli army checkpoint on the road south from Nablus in the West Bank, 2006

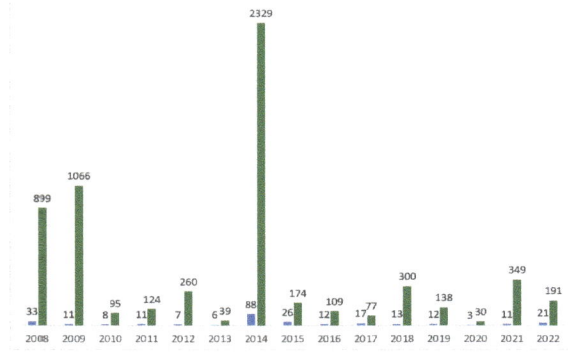

Data from the United Nations: The green line shows Palestinian deaths; the blue line shows Israeli deaths

97

CHAPTER 8

The split between Fatah and Hamas

Fatah's flag: two rifles cross over an image of Palestine; the Arabic in the black banner is "the Palestinian National Liberation Movement" (the full name of Fatah); the Arabic at the bottom of the flag is "revolution until victory".

Hamas' emblem: the mosque at the centre is the Dome of the Rock in Jerusalem; two Palestinian flags frame the mosque; the Arabic on the flags is the Shahada: "There is no god but Allah" and "Muhammad is the messenger of Allah"; the Arabic on the green banner is "the Islamic Resistance Movement" (the full name of Hamas).

Fatah was founded in the late 1950s as a political movement to liberate Palestine. A new generation of young Palestinians, both Muslim and Christian, angry at the daily humiliations of life in makeshift refugee camps, realized they had to forge their own destiny. They chose a policy of armed resistance as the strategy most likely to liberate Palestine and rebuild the Palestinian national consciousness. In January 1965, Fatah launched its first attack on Israel. Three years later at the Battle of Karameh, it became the first Arab army to defeat an Israeli army. Fatah rode on the wave of public support from these attacks to leadership of the Palestinian Liberation Organisation.

'Today, the Arab people of Palestine have decided to take their destiny into their own hands. Today, with arms and courage they are restoring their own lost dignity. Tomorrow, following a long tenacious struggle at the cost of many martyrs, - a struggle which will undoubtedly have the support of the entire Arab liberation movement and the progressive peoples of the world - they will restore their beloved homeland, Palestine. Al-Fatah and the entire Palestinian people wholly believe in their just cause and their ultimate victory. And they also know that on the day the flag of Palestine is hoisted over their freed, democratic, peaceful land, a new era will begin in which the Palestinian Jews will again live in harmony, side by side with the original owners of the land, the Arab Palestinians.'

Press Release number 1 issued by Fatah, 1 January 1968

'Fateh was encouraged by the rapid growth of its trained manpower. A total of 422 volunteers had travelled from Europe, for example, to receive training in guerrilla warfare in Algeria, before being flown to Syria for active service. A constant flow of new recruits from the West Bank also arrived at the Hama camp near Damascus, and Fateh was later to claim that it had trained 'thousands' by the end of the year.'

In August 1967, Fatah announced the start of combat operations in occupied Palestinian territory. Yezid Sayigh, a Palestinian historian, describes a consequence.

The origins of Hamas lie in the Muslim Brotherhood. The Brotherhood was a welfare organisation that believed education was the key to achieving a modern Islamic society. After the Nakba in 1948, the Brotherhood provided vital services for the Palestinian refugees. Yet it was denied a voice in Palestinian affairs for decades. The Egyptian government, during its rule of the Gaza Strip, persecuted the Brotherhood. After 1967, Fatah, the dominant Palestinian party, favoured a secular ideology. In 1987, the Muslim Brotherhood decided the time had come for it to make its voice heard. The PLO claimed to represent the Palestinian people but it had achieved little to alleviate the grinding Israeli occupation inside Palestine. Meanwhile the Iranian revolution in 1979 and the success of Hezbollah in Lebanon showed how powerful Islam could be in rallying resistance to oppression. The Palestinian people rose up in anger at their situation after an Israeli Defence Force truck killed four Palestinians on 8th December 1987. Consequently, the Brotherhood founded an offshoot called Hamas (an acronym for an Arabic phrase meaning Islamic national resistance movement). Hamas committed to an armed struggle to liberate all of Palestine, leading to developing an Islamic society.

'Nationalism, from the point of view of the Islamic Resistance Movement, is part of the religious creed. Nothing in nationalism is more significant or deeper than in the case when an enemy should tread Moslem land. Resisting and quelling the enemy become the individual duty of every Moslem, male or female. A woman can go out to fight the enemy without her husband's permission, and so does the slave: without his master's permission.

Nothing of the sort is to be found in any other regime. This is an undisputed fact. If other nationalist movements are connected with materialistic, human or regional causes, nationalism of the Islamic Resistance Movement has all these elements as well as the more important elements that give it soul and life. It is connected to the source of spirit and the granter of life, hoisting in the sky of the homeland the heavenly banner that joins earth and heaven with a strong bond.'

Article 12, Hamas Covenant in which Hamas set out its identity, positions and aims on 18 August 1988

'Ahmed Yassin is an unlikely leader. Twisted awkwardly in a rusting wheelchair, his tiny body racked by a fit of coughing, he explains quietly why, in the name of Islam, the Palestinians must maintain their armed struggle against Israel.

Despite his frail appearance, Sheikh Yassin speaks with an authority based on unshakeable faith. "If we want a Palestinian state we must have Palestinian land" he insists. "There is no point in making a state on paper. Our state will be Islamic." '

Interview with Sheikh Yassin by The Guardian, 8 September 1988

Fatah continued the armed resistance in the face of Israel's assassinations, imprisonments, and exile. This strategy paid off in raising awareness of the Palestinian cause. In 1974, Fatah received international recognition when its leader, Yasser Arafat, was invited to address the UN. Arafat offered the olive branch of peace or the gun of war. He urged the delegates not to let the olive branch slip from his hand. However, Israel continued to intensify its occupation of Palestine and so Fatah continued to lead the armed struggle to liberate Palestine. From its origins in the refugee camps, Fatah had remained steadfast in this struggle from outside Palestine. By the 1970s, Fatah's base was Lebanon. Israel invaded Lebanon in 1982, forcing Fatah into exile in Tunisia.

'Yasser Arafat's speech was interrupted nine times by applause. When he finished, a large part of the Assembly gave him a standing ovation that lasted nearly two minutes before during and after Mr. Arafat's speech led by Arab delegates. Black Africans and representatives from other third-world countries joined them. Most West European delegates remained reserved throughout.

Mr. Arafat seemed to enjoy what Arabs here called his "triumph" placing an arm over the backrest of a beige armchair that had been placed to the right side of the rostrums.

The armchair is a United Nations status symbol usually reserved for heads of states.'

Arafat negotiates a ceasefire with King Hussein of Jordan, mediated by President Nasser of Egypt, 27 September 1970

New York Times' article covering Yasser Arafat's speech, dated 14 November 1974 and titled 'Dramatic Session'

102

In addition to Israeli hostility, Hamas had to struggle in the face of attempts by Fatah to crush opposition. Fatah signed the Oslo Accords in 1993. Seduced by the trappings of power and patronage, Fatah sacrificed the Palestinian people's rights to their ancient homeland for some empty promises from Israel. The Palestinian people rose up to protest at the Israeli invasion of the al-Aqsa Mosque in Jerusalem, the most holy Islamic site in Palestine, in September 2000. This uprising, known as the al-Aqsa Intifada, lasted until 2005. Israel rejected Hamas's ceasefires and in 2004 killed Hamas' spiritual leader, Sheikh Ahmed Yassin as he was taken from early morning prayers in his wheelchair.

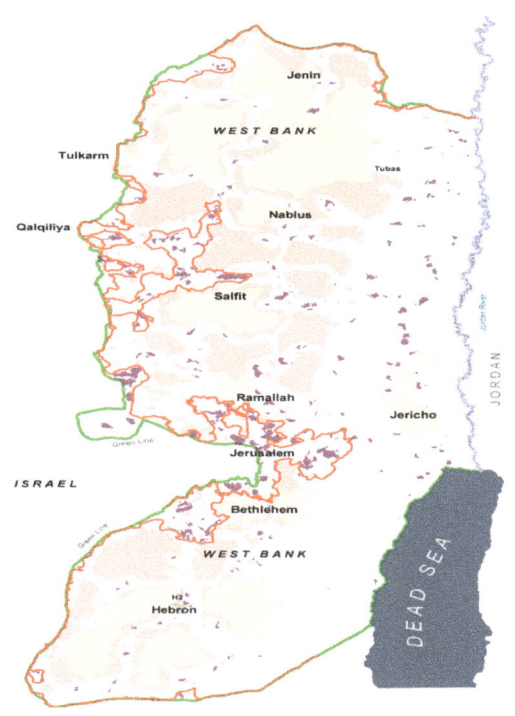

The Oslo Accords divided the West Bank into Area A (full civil and security control by the Palestinian Authority) in yellow, Area B (Palestinian civil control and joint Israeli-Palestinian security control) in pink, and Area C (full Israeli control) in the rest of the West Bank. The purple areas show Israeli settlements. The red line shows the projection of the Wall on 20 February 2005

'We give the Zionist street an opportunity to say its word, to demand from its government to stop terrorism, murder, assassinations... and to withdraw from our land. In return, we will stop all martyrdom and armed operations in the occupied land of 1948.'

Joint press release by the armed wing of Hamas, the al-Qassam brigades, and the al-Aqsa brigades, an armed group connected to Fatah, 5 June 2001

Arafat though came good on his commitment to lay down the gun of war when Israel finally recognised the PLO. In 1987, the Palestinian people rebelled against the Israeli occupation in the First Intifada. Arafat seized the chance to pursue Palestinian statehood through diplomatic, rather than military, means. The Intifada and American pressure forced Israel to the negotiating table. Arafat and the Israeli Prime Minister, Yitzhak Rabin, signed the first Oslo Accord on 13 September 1993. Consequently, Fatah returned to Palestine to lead the newly created Palestinian National Authority.

'Despite the historical injustice inflicted on the Palestinian Arab people resulting in their dispersion and depriving them of their right to self-determination, following upon U.N. General Assembly Resolution 181 (1947), which partitioned Palestine into two states, one Arab, one Jewish, yet it is this Resolution that still provides those conditions of international legitimacy that ensure the right of the Palestinian Arab people to sovereignty.'

Extract from the Palestinian Declaration of Independence proclaimed by Yasser Arafat on 15 November 1988. For Fatah, this extract represents an acceptance of the partition of Palestine into a Palestinian and Israeli state.

Yasser Arafat and Yitzhak Rabin, Israel's Prime Minister, with Bill Clinton, US President, at the White House on 13 September 1993 after the signing of the first Oslo Accords.

The Palestinian people understood by 2005 that the Israeli promises at Oslo were meaningless and that corruption in Fatah had sapped its will to fight for the Palestinian people. Hamas stepped into the political vacuum and won the elections of 2006 for the Palestinian Legislative Council. Mahmoud Abbas, the president of the Palestinian Authority, rejected the democratic will of the Palestinian people. 600 Palestinians were killed in the subsequent civil war between January 2006 and July 2007.

'The al-Aqsa intifada has created new realities on the ground. It has made the Oslo program a thing of the past. All parties, including the Zionist occupiers, now refer to the demise of Oslo. Our people today are more united, more aware, and stronger than before. Hamas is entering these elections after having succeeded, with God's help, in affirming its line of resistance and in ingraining it deep in the hearts of our people.'

Hamas electoral platform announced in Autumn 2005

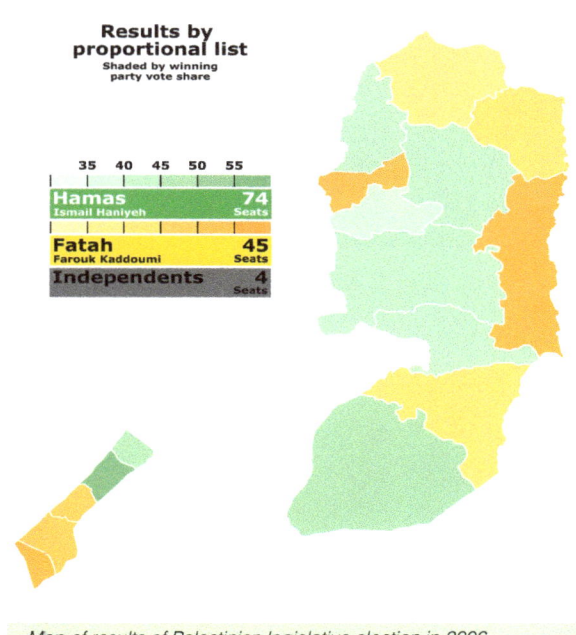

Map of results of Palestinian legislative election in 2006

105

Israel however had no intention of allowing the creation of an independent Palestinian state. It frustrated further negotiations. When the Palestinian people rose up in protest in the Second Intifada in 2000, Israel reinvaded the West Bank and Gaza and destroyed the governing infrastructure which Fatah had built. Using a divide and rule strategy, Israel then unilaterally withdrew Jewish settlers from Gaza in 2005 and resettled them in the West Bank. In the chaos that followed, Hamas, a new religious party, seized power in Gaza in 2007.

Photo of the wall between Abu Dis and Jerusalem, June 2004. Israel began building the wall in 2002 during the Second Intifada.

'The supreme goal of the national liberation cause, led by the Palestinian Liberation Organization (PLO), the sole legitimate representative of the Palestinian people, is to end the occupation, establish a sovereign and independent state on the 1967 borders with Jerusalem as its capital, and reach a just and agreed solution for Palestinian refugees... The Palestinian government is struggling determinedly against a hostile occupation regime, employing all of its energies and available resources, most especially the capacities of our people, to complete the process of building institutions of the independent State of Palestine in order to establish a de facto state apparatus within the next two years.'

Quote by Shlomo Ben Ami, Israeli Foreign Minister, on Democracy Now!, 14 February 2006

Hamas seized control of Gaza in June 2007. Israel imposed an air, sea and land blockade on Gaza to contain Hamas. The blockade turned Gaza into a prison. Hamas' resistance, including firing rockets into Israel, increased its importance as leaders of the Palestinian struggle against the Israeli occupation. The military leadership of Hamas in Gaza became more and more independent from its political leadership in Qatar. At the same time, the world forgot about the Palestinian people. Even Arab countries began to make agreements with Israel and accept its occupation of Palestine. The Fatah-led Palestinian Authority continued to compromise with the Israeli occupation. It also continued to fail to hold elections.

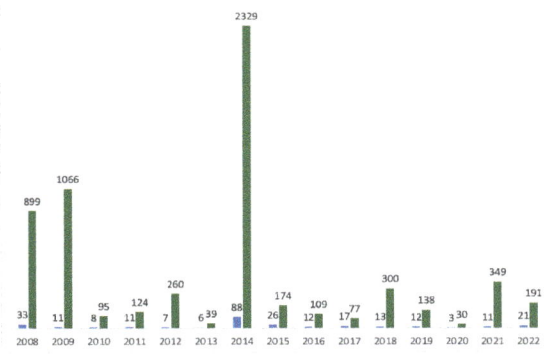

Data from the United Nations: The green line shows Palestinian deaths; the blue line shows Israeli deaths

Hamas Covenant, 1988:
'The Islamic Resistance Movement believes that the land of Palestine is an Islamic Waqf consecrated for future Moslem generations until Judgement Day. It, or any part of it, should not be squandered: it, or any part of it, should not be given up. Neither a single Arab country nor all Arab countries, neither any king or president, nor all the kings and presidents, neither any organization nor all of them, be they Palestinian or Arab, possess the right to do that. Palestine is an Islamic Waqf land consecrated for Moslem generations until Judgement Day.'

Hamas Charter, 2017:
'Hamas believes that no part of the land of Palestine shall be compromised or conceded, irrespective of the causes, the circumstances and the pressures and no matter how long the occupation lasts. Hamas rejects any alternative to the full and complete liberation of Palestine, from the river to the sea. However, without compromising its rejection of the Zionist entity and without relinquishing any Palestinian rights, Hamas considers the establishment of a fully sovereign and independent Palestinian state, with Jerusalem as its capital along the lines of the 4th of June 1967, with the return of the refugees and the displaced to their homes from which they were expelled, to be a formula of national consensus.'

Hamas issued a new charter in May 2017. This source compares Article 13 of the 1988 Covenant and Article 20 of the 2017 Charter.

Fatah continues to enjoy support for pursuing a diplomatic solution. After the death of Yasser Arafat, the Fatah candidate, Mahmoud Abbas, won the presidential election in 2005. More recently, in the run-up to the latest attempted legislative elections in 2021, Fatah was consistently the party which enjoyed the most support in polling of the Palestinian people. However, Fatah continues to be frustrated in this pursuit. Successive Israeli governments have undermined a two-state solution. Hamas continues to be intransigent, and Arab neighbouring states are indifferent. The 2021 elections were delayed because Israel refused to allow Palestinians living in East Jerusalem to vote, and Hamas walked out of the talks. On 7 October 2023 Hamas launched an attack on Israel without consulting other Palestinian leaders. Israel has responded with catastrophic devastation of Gaza and killing of tens of thousands of Palestinians.

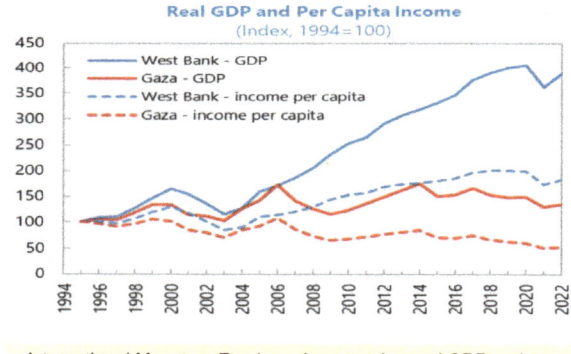

Real GDP and Per Capita Income
(Index, 1994 = 100)
- West Bank - GDP
- Gaza - GDP
- West Bank - income per capita
- Gaza - income per capita

International Monetary Fund graph comparing real GDP and per capita income in the West Bank and Gaza

Polling of voting intention in legislative elections
The election was scheduled for 22 May 2021

Dates of poll	Vote for Fatah	Vote for Hamas
14 - 19 March 2021	43%	30%
8 - 11 December 2020	38%	34%
9 - 12 September 2020	38%	34%
7 - 20 June 2020	36%	34%
5 - 8 February 2020	38%	32%
11 - 14 December 2019	40%	32%
11 - 14 September 2019	38%	29%
7 - 30 June 2019	39%	30%
13 - 16 March 2019	39%	32%

Polling carried out by the Palestinian Center for Policy and Survey Research
Average sample size: 1240

Polling of Palestinians in the run-up to the proposed legislative election in 2021

On 7th October 2023, Hamas broke free from this containment. It stated that it sought, through its surprise attack, to capture Israeli soldiers to achieve a prisoner exchange, to respond to attacks on Palestinians in the West Bank and the al-Aqsa mosque, and to put the Palestinian cause at the centre of world politics.

UNICEF MENA report on the Gaza Strip in 2022

- Unemployment levels in Gaza are amongst the highest in the world: the Q1 jobless rate in 2022 was 46.6%.
- 31% of households in Gaza have difficulties meeting essential education needs such as tuition fees and books.
- 1.3 million out of 2.1 million Palestinians in Gaza (62%) require food assistance.
- At its current operating capacity, the Gaza Power Plant is meeting about 50% of the electricity demand. In 2021, rolling power cuts averaged 11 hours per day.
- 78% of piped water in Gaza is unfit for human consumption.

UNICEF is the United Nations Children's Emergency Fund

Polling of voting intention in legislative elections

Dates of poll	Vote for Fatah	Vote for Hamas
5 - 10 March 2024	22%	47%
22 November - 2 December 2023	19%	51%
6 - 9 September 2023	34%	36%
7 - 11 June 2023	31%	34%
8 - 11 March 2023	35%	33%

Polling carried out by the Palestinian Center for Policy and Survey Research
Average sample size: 1240

Polling of Palestinians

CHAPTER 9

Stasis, Division and Conflict

2008-2024

Internal divisions and improvements in external relations marked the decade in Israel leading up to the attack on October 7th, 2023. Internally, there were worrying divisions over the authority of the Supreme Court. Externally, Iran and its proxies Hezbollah and the Houthi presented a serious threat but paradoxically this shared view of Iran helped draw Israel closer to the UAE, Bahrain, Sudan, and Morocco. The peace process with the Palestinians had ground to a halt because there was no partner for peace. Fatah, the Palestinian leadership in the West Bank, was unpopular, corrupt, and lacked democratic legitimacy as it had refused to hold any elections since 2006. Hamas, the Palestinian leadership in Gaza, continued to deny Israel's right to exist, and refused to cooperate with Fatah. Rocket attacks from Gaza on southern Israel were punished by air strikes on selected terror targets, or if merited, larger operations like Operation Cast Lead in 2008, Pillar of Defence in 2012, and Protective Edge in 2014.

Protesters demonstrating against Netanyahu's plans to suppress the Supreme Court block Ayalon Highway in Tel Aviv, 9th March 2023

US and Israeli delegations meet in Morocco with King Mohammed VI, December 2020

By 2023 the land, air, and sea blockade of Gaza imposed by Israel was entering its seventeenth year and showed no signs of lessening. The Israeli army had attacked Gaza in 2008, 2012, 2014 and 2021, in the process killing thousands and destroying hundreds of homes, mosques, hospitals and clinics. Palestinian leadership in Gaza led by Hamas, a religious party, organised occasional action against Israeli forces, often in response to Israeli attacks on the al-Aqsa Mosque in Jerusalem. Meanwhile Palestinian leadership in the West Bank led by Fatah, a nationalist party, pursued a strategy of collaboration with Israeli forces. This cooperative posture had achieved nothing in terms of preventing Israeli settlers from attacking Palestinian farmers and seizing their lands and crops.

UNICEF MENA report on the Gaza Strip in 2022

- Unemployment levels in Gaza are amongst the highest in the world: the Q1 jobless rate in 2022 was 46.6%.
- 31% of households in Gaza have difficulties meeting essential education needs such as tuition fees and books,
- 1.3 million out of 2.1 million Palestinians in Gaza (62%) require food assistance.
- At its current operating capacity, the Gaza Power Plant is meeting about 50% of the electricity demand. In 2021, rolling power cuts averaged 11 hours per day.
- 78% of piped water in Gaza is unfit for human consumption.

UNICEF is the United Nations Children's Emergency Fund

A burnt-out car in the West Bank after an attack by Israeli settlers in February 2023

113

With its attention distracted, the IDF failed to detect the planning of the Oct 7th attack. Israeli forces were initially overwhelmed – about 1200 people were killed, the majority of whom were civilians, over 200 hostages were taken and there were multiple reports of sexual violence. Israeli governments have a strict doctrine that any attack on Jews must be punished to deter future attacks. Israel was born in the shadow of the Holocaust and the murder of six million Jews. Therefore, October 7th was very traumatic for both Israelis and Jews around the world, as it rocked their confidence in Israel as a place of safety for all Jews.

Map showing, in purple, how far Palestinian militants invaded Israel on 7 to 8 October 2023

Bodies of Hamas militants and houses destroyed after the Be'eri massacre 7 October 2023

Internationally, the Palestinians were more isolated than ever. Israel had strengthened diplomatic relations with several Arab countries in the Gulf. The USA, Israel's long-term protector and enabler, abandoned any pretence of an even-handed approach when it transferred the US embassy from Tel Aviv to Jerusalem in 2018. Extremist Jewish settlers, with the protection of Israeli authorities, continuously stirred up trouble by undermining Palestinian control of the al-Aqsa Mosque. In April 2023 Israeli police raided the Mosque in riot gear, beat Palestinian worshippers and arrested hundreds.

'This agreement does absolutely not serve the Palestinian cause; it rather serves the Zionist narrative. This agreement encourages the occupation [by Israel] to continue its denial of the rights of our Palestinian people, and even to continue its crimes against our people.'

Hazem Qassem, Hamas spokesman in a statement

'The Palestinian leadership rejects and denounces the UAE, Israeli and US trilateral, surprising announcement. [The deal was] a betrayal of Jerusalem, al-Aqsa, and the Palestinian cause.'

Nabil Abu Rudeineh, spokesman Palestinian President, Mahmoud Abbas

Palestinian response to news of the normalisation of relations between Israel and the UAE, 16 August 2020

'We warn that desecrating the sanctity of al-Aqsa Mosque is playing with fire [...] Not allowing worshippers to perform their religious duties and their rituals in this holy month and restricting freedom to enter the al-Aqsa Mosque, all that pushes towards an explosive situation which is what we are warning about [...] Ramadan comes with Gaza bombed by Israel and women unable to find food for their children and five months that have passed with the world failing to preserve human dignity.'

Ayman Safadi, Jordan's Foreign Minister, speaking at a press conference in Amman, March 11, 2024

Despite its overwhelming military superiority, the IDF found itself at a disadvantage in fighting Hamas which was dug into an extensive tunnel system under Gaza. Hamas routinely used its own population as civilian shields and was embedded in Gaza's hospitals. To reduce civilian casualties, the IDF has held back from the full use of its superior firepower even though this decision exposed Israeli soldiers to the greater risks of house to house fighting with Hamas terrorists.

'Hamas, [...] has been using human shields in conflicts with Israel since 2007 [...] The strategic logic of human shields has two components. It is based on an awareness of Israel's desire to minimise collateral damage [...] If the IDF uses lethal force and causes an increase in civilian casualties, Hamas can utilise that as a lawfare tool: it can accuse Israel of committing war crimes, which could result in the imposition of a wide array of sanctions. Alternatively, if the IDF limits its use of military force in Gaza to avoid collateral damage, Hamas will be less susceptible to Israeli attacks. [...] Moreover, despite the Israeli public's high level of support for the Israeli political and military leadership during operations, civilian casualties are one of the friction points between Israeli left-wing and right-wing supporters, with the former questioning the outcomes of the operation.'

NATO Strategic Communications Centre of Excellence, report on Hamas' use of Human Shields 2014

Posters in Tel Aviv calling for the return of Israeli hostages in Gaza

The attack launched by Hamas on Israel on October 7th was in response to the desecration of the al-Aqsa Mosque earlier in the year, according to Hamas military leadership. Hamas forces broke out of the Gaza enclave and attacked Israeli Defence Force positions, soldiers and reservists. They captured prisoners who were brought back to Gaza as hostages to exchange for the thousands of Palestinian prisoners held in Israeli jails without trial.

A bulldozer breaks through the Israeli barrier in northern Gaza on October 7 2023

'Over the last month we have witnessed a significant spike in Israel's use of administrative detention - detention without charge or trial that can be renewed indefinitely - which was already at a 20 year high before the latest escalation in hostilities on 7 October. [...] Testimonies and video evidence also point to numerous incidents of torture and other ill-treatment by Israeli forces including severe beatings and deliberate humiliation of Palestinians who are detained in dire conditions.'

Heba Morayef, Amnesty Regional Director for MENA
November 8, 2023

The attack from Gaza has rallied Israeli society around both the need to defeat Hamas and to care for the thousands of civilians evacuated from their homes on Israel's southern and northern borders. In addition, the pro-Palestinian demonstrations which erupted across the world – in some cases within a couple of days of the attack – were a reminder that the scourge of anti-Semitism was never far beneath the surface, even in supposedly liberal democracies, and Jews cannot depend on the kindness of others. More recently concerns that the government has done too little to bring home hostages has eroded this national unity. There have been widespread protests about how the Netanyahu government has conducted the war.

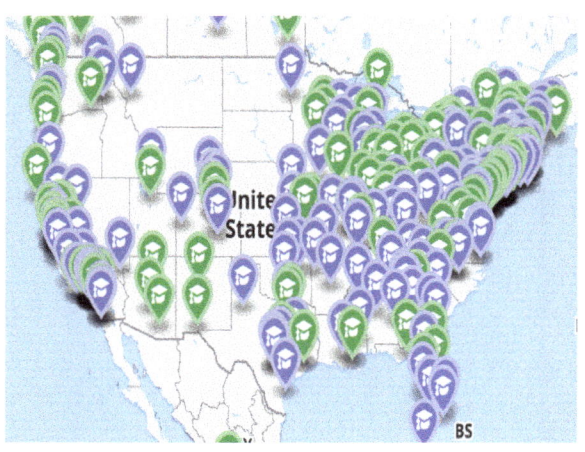

Map showing the extent of protests against the Israel Hamas war across the USA.

'Operation Swords of Iron, the official Israeli name for the war that erupted on the Southern and Northern fronts on October 7, caused the government to order the evacuation of communities adjacent to the front lines [...] around 253,000 Israelis had been evacuated from their homes. Of them, around 94,000 were [...] moved to another community; some 88,000 were relocated to hotels; and around 70,000 made their own arrangements. This is the largest civilian evacuation in Israel's history.'

Extract from Institute of National Security Studies report on 'The evacuation of Israeli Communities During the Swords of Iron War'.

Israelis had grown used to the idea that they could live comfortably in a country of seven million Jews which systematically controlled and oppressed roughly the same number of Arabs, and that there would be no price to pay. The October 7th attack caught the Israelis by surprise and shattered that illusion. The Israeli retaliation was indiscriminate and ferocious. By December, Israel had dropped US supplied munitions equivalent to two nuclear bombs on the civilian population of Gaza. In June 2024 the death toll reached 36,000 and the majority of those killed were women and children. Over 50% of all buildings in Gaza were destroyed, and the population was on the brink of famine. In the West Bank and East Jerusalem over 430 Palestinians had been killed. As world opinion turned against this senseless carnage Israel responded by killing more journalists (over 95 were killed in Gaza between October and May) and shutting down the main Arab news organization, Al Jazeera.

IDF forces in a destroyed neighbourhood in the Gaza Strip at the start of November 2023.

 BritishRedCross

"Over 1.5 million people are sheltering in Rafah, many living on the streets in makeshift shelters, with little access to food and water, and other essentials. Our colleagues at the Palestine Red Crescent Society are working tirelessly - from delivering emergency health assistance, to facilitating aid deliveries. But the reality is that we need a significant increase in humanitarian aid to match the needs. [...] People's lives are hanging in the balance."

Rory Moylan, British Red Cross' Head of MENA, May 17th, 2024

British Red Cross is an international Humanitarian Aid organisation

It's just over a century since the international community recognised the Jewish right to a home in the ancient land of Israel and Judah, and seventy-five years since Jews established a state of their own and defended it against attacks from their neighbours. Israelis remain committed to maintaining their ancient homeland as a place of refuge for Jews anywhere in the world and are proud to live in the one prosperous democracy in a region riven by war, sectarian strife, and autocracy.

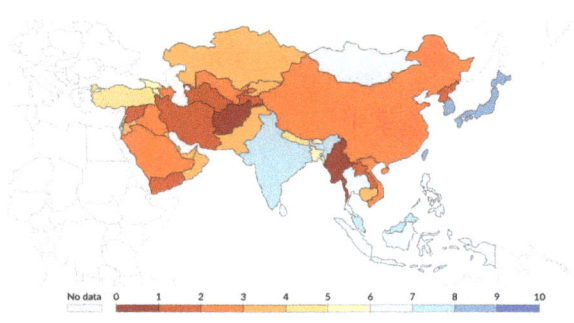

Israel is the only country in the Middle East categorised as a democracy by the Economist Intelligence Unit

The Merneptah Victory Stele, dated 1209 BCE from the Egyptian Museum in Cairo. While alternative translations exist, the majority of biblical archeologists translate a set of hieroglyphs as "Israel", representing the first instance of the name Israel in the historical record.

It's just over a century since a British government began to promote the resettlement of central European Jews fleeing Russian pogroms onto land belonging to Arab Palestinians. The Zionist settlers have always had maximalist goals. From the start they wanted to take all the land between the Mediterranean and the River Jordan for themselves alone, and they have not wavered from their goal. Palestinians remain steadfast in their commitment to defend their ancestral homelands and sacred religious sites from European settler colonialism.

Part of the al-Aqsa Mosque in the Old City of Jerusalem, the third holiest site in Islam.

This key outside the city of Jericho in the West Bank is one of many found in Palestine. The key symbolises Palestinians' determination to return to their lost homes.

Author's thanks
Michael Davies, July 2024

This book is part of a project to change the way we study history and it draws on many sources of inspiration. In 2004 Professor Eyal Naveh and Professor Sami Adwan, with Israeli and Palestinian colleagues, working under the auspices of the Peace Research Institute in the Middle East (PRIME) wrote a joint history textbook called *Side by Side.* This book sank in Israel and Palestine but had a healthy afterlife in universities around the rest of the world. I am grateful to Professor Naveh for his early encouragement when I first approached him with my idea, and since then for his continued support. I would also thank Assistant Professor Abdalkarim Zawawi at An-Najah University, Associate Professor Hillel Cohen at Hebrew University, and Professor Colette Mazzucelli at New York University for helping me experiment with dual narrative teaching in their classrooms.

I am also grateful to Lancaster Royal Grammar School in the UK. It was here, working closely with Hugh Castle and the rest of his team over several years, that many of the best ideas about using dual narratives to teach history were incubated. Also, Dr Chris Pyle, the headteacher, deserves thanks for the support he gave to a seminal school trip Hugh and I took to both Israel and the West Bank. Chris and Hugh embraced the idea that education may well mean students finding themselves in uncomfortable and unfamiliar places.

Julian Richer who co-founded Parallel Histories with me saw the need for better education about Israel and the West Bank. He contacted me out of the blue in 2015 after reading an article in *The Guardian* about the school trip I took to Israel and the West Bank. He has been a constant support since then and his advice has been invaluable on many occasions. The Churchill Fellowship provided early support for the concept and Randolph and Jack Churchill have remained enthusiastically involved. Thanks to Lord Turnberg who sponsored our conferences in the House of Lords, and Robbie Butler, Deputy Leader of the Ulster Unionist Party, and Ben McPherson MSP who have done the same in Stormont and Holyrood. Thanks also to our patron, Jonathan Powell, and our Chair of Trustees Tim Ramsey MBE for their enthusiasm and endorsement and our wonderful board of trustees.

Many thanks to Ayelet and Edo Segal at Touchcast in New York for their interactive video software and storage. The generosity of friends and relations is always a fillip – it puts a smile on my face every time the donation alert pings on my phone.

Many people have commented on the quality of the design behind the Parallel Histories brand and that's all down to Marcus Hewitt and Susan Hopper at yellow.design in New York City and Los Angeles. They created the Parallel Histories brand and the identity for all our products.

This book has been through many iterations over the years and is the product of many people's effort and expertise. The parts that shine are our communal efforts and any mistakes are mine. I'd like to thank David Garrett and Michelle Kass and Jim Rose for their advice on copyright and licensing. And thank you to my sisters Rosamond and Geraldine who proof read and checked the manuscript. But the most important acknowledgement of all is to Joshua Hillis, my completely invaluable Deputy Editor for the last five years.

I know that this dual narrative approach to learning about Israel and Palestine works, because it's been tried and tested in thousands of classrooms around the world. Therefore, I owe a huge debt of gratitude to all the teachers we work with in sixty countries who are brave and determined enough to teach controversial topics when they are not compulsory. Their ideas for new programs, suggestions for improvements to existing ones and reports on student progress are invaluable. And of course, the team at Parallel Histories UK, Meredith Cann, Hugh Castle, and Tim Leadbetter for all of whom this is a labour of love.

Suggested reading

If you would like to read more about the history of the conflict, this is a selection of books which offer a range of interpretations:

Tareq Baconi, *Hamas Contained: The Rise and Pacification of Palestinian Resistance*
Hillel Cohen, *Year Zero of the Arab-Israeli Conflict: 1929*
Sami Hadawi, *Bitter Harvest: A Modern History of Palestine*
Efraim Karsh, *Palestine Betrayed*
Rashid Khalidi, *Palestinian Identity: The Construction of Modern National Consciousness*
Rashid Khalidi, *The Hundred Years' War on Palestine: A History of Settler Colonialism and Resistance, 1917-2017*
Nur Masalha, *Palestine: A Four Thousand Year History*
Benny Morris, *Righteous Victims: A History of the Zionist-Arab Conflict 1881-1999*
Benny Morris, *1948: A History of the First Arab-Israeli War*
Sari Nusseibeh, *Once Upon a Country: A Palestinian Life*
Edward Said, *The Politics of Dispossession: The Struggle for Palestinian Self-Determination, 1969-1994*
Rosemary Sayigh, *Voices: Palestinian Women Narrate Displacement*
Yezid Sayigh, *Armed Struggle and the Search for State: the Palestinian National Movement, 1949-1993*
Simon Sebag Montefiore, *Jerusalem: The Biography*
Tom Segev, *1949: The First Israelis*
Tom Segev, *One Palestine, Complete: Jews and Arabs Under the British Mandate*
Tom Segev, *1967: Israel, the War, and The Year that Transformed the Middle East*
Anita Shapira, *Israel: A History*
Avi Shlaim, *The Iron Wall: Israel and the Arab World*

Acknowledgements and attributions

CHAPTER 1

Chapter photo: David Lisbona / Dafna Kaplan / Flickr / CC BY 2.0. Accessible here: https://Acknowledgements .flickr.com/photos/dlisbona/73870615

Source 1: Emmanuelm / Wikimedia / CC BY 3.0. Accessible here: https://commons.wikimedia.org/wiki/File:Map_Land_of_Israel.jpg

Source 2: Public domain. Estimates by Sergio DellaPergola (2001), drawing on the work of Bachi (1975). Figures in thousands. Accessible here: https://en.wikipedia.org/wiki/Demographic_history_of_Palestine_(region)#:~:text=He%20writes%3A%20%22...,have%20been%20less%20considering%20population

Source 3: Public domain. Estimates by Sergio DellaPergola (2001), drawing on the work of Bachi (1975). Figures in thousands. Accessible here: https://en.wikipedia.org/wiki/Demographic_history_of_Palestine_(region)#:~:text=He%20writes%3A%20%22...,have%20been%20less%20considering%20population

Source 4: Public domain. DieBuche / Wikipedia. Accessible here: https://en.m.wikipedia.org/wiki/File:Map_of_expansion_of_Caliphate.svg

Source 5: Public domain. United Kingdom Government signed by Arthur Balfour / British Library / Wikimedia. Accessible here: https://en.wikipedia.org/wiki/File:Balfour_declaration_unmarked.jpg

Source 6: Public domain. National Photo Collection of Israel, Photography dept. Goverment Press Office, under the digital ID D131-027 / Wikimedia. Accessible here: https://sr.wikipedia.org/wiki/%D0%94%D0%B0%D1%82%D0%BE%D1%82%D0%B5%D0%BA%D0%B0:THEODOR_HERZL_AT_THE_FIRST_ZIONIST_CONGRESS_IN_BASEL_ON_25.8.1897._%D7%AA%D7%90%D7%95%D7%93%D7%95%D7%A8_%D7%94%D7%A8%D7%A6%D7%9C_%D7%91%D7%A7%D7%95%D7%A0%D7%92%D7%A8%D7%A1_%D7%94%D7%A6%D7%99%D7%95%D7%A0%D7%99_%D7%94%D7%A8%D7%90%D7%A9%D7%95%D7%9F_-_1897.8.25.jpg

Source 7: Produced by Parallel Histories.

Source 8: Public domain. Paul Castelnau / Wikipedia Accessible here: https://en.wikipedia.org/wiki/File:Arab_fighters_akaba.png

Source 9: Public domain. The Migration Museum, London. Accessible here: https://Acknowledgements .migrationmuseum.org/exploring-the-migrant-history-of-victorian-east-london/

Source 10: Public Domain. United States Holocaust Memorial Museum, courtesy of National Archives and Records Administration, College Park, Source Record ID: 306-NT-177-708C, Second Record ID: 306-NT-865-A, bpk-Bildagentur, Copyright: Agency Agreement, Accessible here: https://collections.ushmm.org/search/catalog/pa1067754

Source 11: Public Domain. A Survey of Palestine: prepared in December 1945 and January 1946 for the information of the Anglo-American Committee of Inquiry. Vol. I. 1946. Govt. Printer Palestine, pp. 245. Accessible here: https://Acknowledgements .bjpa.org/content/upload/bjpa/a_su/A%20SURVEY%20OF%20PALESTINE%20DEC%201945-JAN%201946%20VOL%20I.pdf

Source 12: Public Domain. United States Holocaust Memorial Museum, courtesy of National Archives and Records Administration, College Park, Source Record ID: 306-NT-177-708C, Second Record ID: 306-NT-865-A, bpk-Bildagentur, Copyright: Agency Agreement. Accessible here: http://palestineisraelpopulation.blogspot.com/

Source 13: Public domain. Zoltan Kluger / National Photo Collection of Israel, Photography dept. Goverment Press Office (link), under the digital ID D844-005 / Wikimedia. Accessible here: https://commons.wikimedia.org/wiki/File:Flickr_-_Government_Press_Office_%28GPO%29_-_Apartment_houses_damaged_during_the_Egyptian_air_attack_on_Tel_Aviv.jpg

Source 14: Public domain. Department of History, U.S. Military Academy / Wikimedia. Accessible here: https://commons.wikimedia.org/wiki/File:1948_arab_israeli_war_-_May15-June10.jpg

Source 15: Public domain. Fred Csasznik / Front cover of The Birth of the Palestinian Refugee Problem by Benny Morris, Cambridge University Press 1989 / Wikimedia. Accessible here: https://en.wikipedia.org/wiki/File:Palestinian_refugees.jpg

Source 16: Public Domain. Extract taken from IMEU; Plan Dalet: Blueprint for the Ethnic Cleansing of Palestine March 08, 2013 IMEU. Accessible here: https://imeu.org/article/plan-dalet

Source 17: Public domain. Unknown author / US govt. archives / Wikipedia. Accessible here: https://en.wikipedia.org/wiki/File:Camp_David,_Menachem_Begin,_Anwar_Sadat,_1978.jpg

Source 18: Public domain. The Covenant of the Hamas, 1988 — main points, published on Israel's Foreign Ministry's website. Accessible here: https://Acknowledgements .gov.il/en/departments/general/the-covenant-of-the-hamas-main-points

Source 19: Licensed under Creative Commons, Accessible here: https://commons.wikimedia.org/wiki/File:Intifada_erase_slogan.jpg

Source 20: Public domain. Vince Musi / The White House / gpo.gov (https://web.archive.org/web/20061123154643/http://Acknowledgements .access.gpo.gov/nara/pubpaps/1993portv2.html) / Wikimedia. Accessible here: https://commons.wikimedia.org/wiki/File:Bill_Clinton,_Yitzhak_Rabin,_Yasser_Arafat_at_the_White_House_1993-09-13.jpg

Source 21: Avishai Teicher via the PikiWiki - Israel free image collection project (http://Acknowledgements .pikiwiki.org.il?action=gallery&img_id=9565) / Wikimedia / CC-BY-2.5. Accessible here: https://commons.wikimedia.org/wiki/File:PikiWiki_Israel_9565_monument_of_the_meggido_junction_terror_attack_56.jpg

Source 22: Graph published by the Jewish Virtual Library. Available here: https://Acknowledgements .jewishvirtuallibrary.org/background-and-overview-of-israel-s-security-fence

Source 23: Noorrovers / Wikimedia / CC-BY-2.5. Accessible here: https://commons.wikimedia.org/wiki/File:Palestinian-loss-of-land-1946-2010.jpg

Source 24: Handala Cartoon by Naji al-Ali / Olga Berrios / Flickr / CC BY 2.0. Accessible here: https://Acknowledgements .flickr.com/photos/ofernandezberrios/2828572972

CHAPTER 2

Chapter photo: Public domain. Balfour Declaration, United Kingdom Government, signed by Arthur Balfour, British Library. Accessible here: https://commons.wikimedia.org/wiki/File:Balfour_declaration_unmarked.jpg

Source 1: Extract from Tamārī Salīm. 2015. Year of the Locust : A Soldier's Diary and the Erasure of Palestine's Ottoman Past Paperback ed. Berkeley: University of California Press.

Source 2: Public domain. The Times of London, 26 April 1920 / Wikipedia. Accessible here: https://en.wikipedia.org/wiki/File:Zionist_Rejoicings._British_Mandate_For_Palestine_Welcomed,_The_Times,_Monday,_Apr_26,_1920.png

Source 3: Extract from MacMillan Margaret. 2001. Peacemakers : The Paris Conference of 1919 and Its Attempt to End War. London: J. Murray, pp. 392

132

Source 4: Wikimedia / "G. Eric and Edith Matson Photograph Collection," Library of Congress Prints and Photographs Division Washington, D.C., Gift; Episcopal Home; 1978, digital ID matpc.18683 (http://hdl.loc.gov/loc.pnp/matpc.18683).Accessible here: https://commons.wikimedia.org/wiki/File:British_troops_marching_past_Barclay%27s_Bank,_Jerusalem._1938._matpc.18683.jpg

Source 5: Public domain / CC0 1.0. Persecution of the Jews in Russia: Street riots in Kiev, drawing by Oskar E. Wycinekfrom Neue Illustrirte Zeitung 1881, no. 37, p. 596. Polish original: PrześladowanieŻydów AcknowledgementsRosji: Zamieszki uliczne AcknowledgementsKijowie wg rysunku Oskara E. Wycinek z NeueIllustrirte Zeitung 1881, nr. 37, s. 596. Author: Cause, A. Date: 1881. Object Number: MNK III-ryc.-39103. Accessible here: https://Acknowledgements .lookandlearn.com/history-images/YNK1069769/Persecution-of-the-Jews-in-Russia-Street-riots-in-Kiev-drawing-by-Oskar-E-Wycinek-f%E2%80%A6

Source 6: Public domain. War Department. Office of the Assistant Secretary of War. Strategic Services Unit. 9/1945-10/19/1946. National Archives Identifier 6704475. Agency-Assigned Identifier page 34. Accessible here: https://catalog.archives.gov/id/6704475

Source 7: Public domain. Unknown author / Wikimedia. Accessible here: https://commons. wikimedia.org/wiki/File:Bundposter1918.jpg

Source 8: Public domain. Memorandum by Edwin Montagu to the British Cabinet, August 1917. Accessible here: https://balfourproject.org/edwin-montagu-and-zionism-1917/

Source 9: Public domain. Letter from the World Zionist Organisation to the British Foreign Secretary regarding the offer of land in East Africa, 4 September 1903. Viennese writer Theodore Herzl established the first Zionist Congress in 1897. The National Archives, London. Ref: FO 2/785. Details here: https://discovery.nationalarchives.gov.uk/details/r/C1915658

Source 10: Public domain. Emil Flohri / Wikimedia / Library of Congress Prints and Photographs Division Washington, D.C., digital ID ppmsca.05438 (http://hdl.loc.gov/loc.pnp/ppmsca.05438). Accessible here: https://commons.wikimedia.org/wiki/File:1904_Russian_Tsar-Stop_your_cruel_oppression_of_the_Jews-LOC_hh0145s.jpg

Source 11: Palestine: Palestine Royal Commission; minutes of evidence heard at secret sessions, Nov 1936 to May 1937. The National Archives FO 492/19. Details here: https://discovery.nationalarchives.gov.uk/details/r/C1915658

Source 12: Public domain. 'The Stranger at our Gate' Frank Beard, from 'Fifty great cartoons by Frank Beard', 1890. Chicago: Ram's Horn Press / Wikimedia. Accessible here: https://en.wikipedia.org/wiki/History_of_antisemitism_in_the_United_States#/media/File:The_Stranger_at_our_Gate,_by_Frank_Beard.jpg

Source 13: Crown Copyright / Contains public sector information licensed under the Open Government Licence v3.0. CABINET. PALESTINE. MEMORANDUM BY THE SECRETARY OF STATE FOR THE COLONIES. Colonial Office, 11th February, 1923. CAB/24/159. Accessible here: http://filestore.nationalarchives.gov.uk/pdfs/small/cab-24-159-CP-200.pdf

Source 14: Public domain. American Colony . Photo Department, John D Whiting, Lewis Larsson, and G. Eric Matson, photographer. Meetings of British, Arab, and Bedouin officials in Amman, Jordan, April. Jordan Amman, 1921. Photograph. https://Acknowledgements .loc.gov/item/2007675257/. Accessible here: https://loc.getarchive.net/media/meetings-of-british-arab-and-bedouin-officials-in-amman-jordan-april-1921-37

Source 15: Public domain. Accessible here: https://balfourproject.org/translation-of-a-letter-from-mcmahon-to-husayn-october-24-1915/

Source 16: Colonel Cyril Wilson to Cairo (Wingate?), May 24, 1917, Cambridge University, Churchill College, Lloyd Papers, Arabian file, January–June 1917, 9/9. Quoted in Schneer Jonathan. 2010. The Balfour Declaration : The Origins of the Arab-Israeli Conflict. 1st ed. New York: Random House.

Source 17: Public domain. PALESTINE, Statement of Policy, Presented by the Secretary of State for the Cabinet to Parliament, By Command of His Majesty, May 1939. Open Government Licence version 1.0 (OGL v1.0). Contains public sector information licensed under the Open Government Licence v1.0.. Accessible here: https://en.wikipedia.org/wiki/File:1939_White_Paper_cmd_6019.djvu

Source 18: Coins from the years 1922-1948, from the British Mandate of Palestine. In the collection of the Jewish Museum of Switzerland. Object number: JMS 283. Photographer: Dieter Hofer / Wikimedia / CC BY-SA 4.0. Accessible here: https://commons.wikimedia.org/wiki/File:Coins_from_the_British_Mandate_for_Palestine.jpg

Source 19: Public domain. Printed for the War Cabinet. October 1917. SECRET. THE FUTURE OF PALESTINE. CAB/24/30. The Future of Palestine, Lord Curzon's October 1917 cabinet memorandum. Accessible here: http://filestore.nationalarchives.gov.uk/pdfs/large/cab-24-30.pdf

Source 20: Public domain. Al Falastin / Issa El-Issa / Wikimedia. Accessible here: https://en.wikipedia.org/wiki/File:A_1936_caricature_published_in_the_Falastin_newspaper_on_Zionism_and_Palestine.png

CHAPTER 3

Chapter Photo: Public domain / IWM Non Commercial Licence. © IWM E 29957. No 1 Army Film & Photographic Unit, Dallison George (Sgt) / Wikipedia. Accessible here: https://en.wikipedia.org/wiki/File:The_British_Mandate_in_Palestine_1917-1948_E29957.jpg ; https://www.iwm.org.uk/collections/item/object/205196537

Source 1: Public domain. Unknown author / Wikimedia. Accessible here: https://commons.wikimedia.org/wiki/File:Tiger_Hill_(ship)_1939.jpg

Source 3: Extract from Furlonge Geoffrey Warren. 1969. *Palestine Is My Country; the Story of Musa Alami.* New York: Praeger

Source 4: Resolution of a meeting at Nablus on the 18th Anniversary of the Balfour Declaration, 2nd November, 1935. Institute of Palestine Studies.

Source 5: (Above) Public domain. American Colony . Photo Department, photographer. Jewish anti Palestine White Paper demonstrations. Women's demonstration on . Demonstration before the District Offices on the Jaffa Road, taken while one of the young women was emphatically denouncing the new polity. Jerusalem, 1939. Photograph. https://www.loc.gov/item/2019710389/

(Below) American Colony . Photo Department, photographer. Palestine disturbances . Palestine Arabs at Abou Ghosh taking the oath of allegiance to the Arab cause, viz. to fight Jewish immigration, etc. Israel Abu Ghaush, 1936. Photograph. https://www.loc.gov/item/2019708823/

Source 6: Public domain. Palestine; termination of the mandate 15th May, 1948. Author Great Britain. Colonial Office. Publisher London : HMSO. Accessible here: https://commons.wikimedia. org/w/index.php?title=File:Palestine_termination_of_the_mandate_15th_May_1948.djvu

Source 7: Petition from inhabitants of Nablus against Zionist domination in Palestine, The National Archives, London. Ref: FO 608/99/5 Folio no. 370. Details here: https://discovery.nationalarchives. gov.uk/browse/r/h/C9018484

Source 8: Personal correspondence between Sir Henry Gurney, Chief Secretary in Jerusalem and John Martin, Assistant Under-Secretary at Colonial Office, on conditions in Palestine. The National Archives, London. Ref: CO 967/102. Details here: https://discovery.nationalarchives.gov.uk/details/r/ C360244

Source 9: Public domain, out of copyright. National Army Museum, Study collection, London. NAM Accession Number: NAM. 1997-06-54-103. Accessible here: https://collection.nam.ac.uk/detail. php?acc=1997-06-54-103

Source 10: Public domain, out of copyright. 'B' Company sandbagging trucks, Haifa May 1936, From photographs collected by Major H M Cox of the Corps of Military Police in Egypt and Palestine 1943 until 1946. National Army Museum, Study collection, London. NAM Accession Number NAM. 1987-04-11-89. Accessible here: https://collection.nam.ac.uk/detail.php?acc=1987-04-11-89

Source 11: Chaim Kahanov and Zecharia Oryon / Wikimedia. Accessible here: https://commons.wikimedia.org/wiki/File:Train_hostages.jpg

Source 12: American Colony . Photo Department, photographer. Palestine disturbances . Palestine Arabs at Abou Ghosh taking the oath of allegiance to the Arab cause, viz. to fight Jewish immigration, etc. Israel Abu Ghaush, 1936. Photograph. https://www.loc.gov/item/2019708823/

Source 13: Back the Boys with War Savings. Imperial War Museum. © IWM Art.IWM PST 15505. Accessible here: https://www.iwm.org.uk/collections/item/object/32692

Source 14: United States. Department of State. (19391989). The Department of State bulletin. [Washington: Office of Media Services, Bureau of Public Affairs; for sale by Supt. of Docs., U.S. Govt. Print. Off.], pp. 790-791.Accessible here: https://babel.hathitrust.org/cgi/pt?id=uiuo.ark%3A%2F13960%2Ft15m7sm3h&seq=801

Source 15: Public domain. Palestine; termination of the mandate 15th May, 1948. Author Great Britain. Colonial Office. Publisher London : HMSO. Accessible here: https://commons.wikimedia.org/w/index.php?title=File:Palestine_termination_of_the_mandate_15th_May_1948.djvu

Source 16: Clandestine Immigration and Naval Museum, Haifa / Wikimedia / CC BY-SA 3.0. Accessible here: https://commons.wikimedia.org/wiki/File:BritsLvHaifa3061948.jpg

Source 17: Extract from Crossman Richard Howard Stafford. 1947. Palestine Mission a Personal Record Repr ed. London: Hamilton.

Source 18: Public domain. Wikimedia / National Photo Collection of Israel, Photography dept. Goverment Press Office, under the digital ID D410-028 (http://gpophotoeng.gov.il/fotoweb/Grid.fwx?search=D410-028.jpg#Preview1). Accessible here: https://commons.wikimedia.org/wiki/File:May_Day_Tel-Aviv_1949.jpg

Source 19: Public domain. The Future of Palestine (1915) by Herbert Samuel, The National Archives, London, Ref: CAB 37/123/43. Accessible here: https://en.wikisource.org/wiki/The_Future_of_Palestine

Source 20: Public domain. Hansard, Reference list: HC Deb 31 January 1947 vol 432 cc1300-58. Accessible here: https://api.parliament.uk/historic-hansard/commons/1947/jan/31/palestine-jewish-terrorism#S5CV0432P0_19470131_HOC_156

CHAPTER 4

Chapter photo: Public domain. Zoltan Kluger / National Photo Collection of Israel, Photography dept. Goverment Press Office (link), digital ID D820-065 / Wikimedia. Accessible here: https://commons.wikimedia.org/wiki/File:A_GROUP_OF_FORMER_BUCHENWALD_INMATES_ON_BOARD_THE_REFUGEE_SHIP_%22MATAROA%22_IN_HAIFA_PORT._%D7%A0%D7%99%D7%A6%D7%95%D7%9C%D7%99_%D7%A9%D7%95%D7%90%D7%94_%D7%9E%D7%9E%D7%97%D7%A0%D7%94_%D7%91%D7%95%D7%9B%D7%A0%D7%95%D7%95%D7%90%D7%9C%D7%93,_%D7%9E%D7%92%D7%99%D7%A2%D7%99%D7%9D_%D7%9C%D7%A0%D7%9E%D7%9C_%D7%97%D7%99%D7%A4%D7%94.D820-065.jpg

Public domain. Fred Csasznik / Front cover of The Birth of the Palestinian Refugee Problem by Benny Morris, Cambridge University Press 1989 / Wikipedia. Accessible here: https://en.wikipedia.org/wiki/File:Palestinian_refugees.jpg

Source 1: Public domain. Unknown author / Wikipedia. Accessible here: https://en.wikipedia.org/wiki/File:Quartier_commercial_juif_attaqué_-_2_décembre_1947.jpg

Source 2: Extracts from: Morris Benny. 2008. 1948 : A History of the First Arab-Israeli War Book Club ed. New Haven Conneticut: Yale University Press, pp. 50, 70 and Kaufmann Myron S. 1970. The Coming Destruction of Israel. New York: New American Library, pp. 26-27.

Source 3: Public domain. Israeli GPO photographer / National Photo Collection of Israel, Photography dept. Government Press Office (link(http://gpophoto.gov.il/haetonot/Eng_Default.aspx)), under the digital ID D98-121 (http://gpophotoeng.gov.il/fotoweb/Grid.fwx?search=D98-121.jpg#Preview1) / Wikimedia. Accessible here: https://commons.wikimedia.org/wiki/File:Menachem_Begin_při_projevu_v_srpnu_1948.jpg

Source 4: Extract from Finkelstein Norman G. 2003. Image and Reality of the Israel-Palestine Conflict. 2nd ed. London: Verso. pp.86

Source 5: Public Domain. Secret British Police Report Regarding the Situation in Haifa (1948) by A.J. Bidmead for Superintendent of Police, Haifa. Accessible here: https://en.wikisource.org/wiki/Secret_British_Police_Report_Regarding_the_Situation_in_Haifa

Source 6: Extract from Morris Benny. 2004. The Birth of the Palestinian Refugee Problem Revisited. Cambridge: University Press, pp. 139

Source 7: Extract from Morris Benny. 2004. The Birth of the Palestinian Refugee Problem Revisited. Cambridge: University Press, pp. 191

Source 8: Public domain. Unknown author / Wikimedia. Accessible here: https://en.wikipedia.org/wiki/File:KD_1946.JPG

Source 9: Weimar_Republic_1930.svg / Blank_map_of_Europe.svg / Alphathon / Futurist110 / Wikimedia / CC BY-SA 3.0. Accessible here: https://commons.wikimedia.org/wiki/File:Holocaustdeathtoll%25.png

Source 10: Extract from Jewish Refugees from Arab Countries The Case for Rights and Redress by Justice for Jews from Arab Countries (JJAC), which was submitted to the European Parliament in 2006. Accessible here: https://Acknowledgements .europarl.europa.eu/meetdocs/2004_2009/documents/fd/il20062006_07/il20062006_07en.pdf

Source 11: Adapted from: Before Their Diaspora, Institute for Palestinian Studies 1984. Based on ACKNOWLEDGEMENTS .Khalidi, Ed. From Haven to Conquest Institute for Palestinian Studies Washington, D.C., 1971. Palestinian Academic Society for the Study of International Affairs (PASSIA). Accessible here: 188.166.160.81/passia_old/passia.org/palestine_facts/MAPS/newpdf/Zionistmilitaryoperations.gif

Source 12: Extract from Flapan, Simha. "The Palestinian Exodus of 1948." Journal of Palestine Studies 16, no. 4 (1987): 3–26.

Source 13: Bundesarchiv, Bild 146-1987-004-09A / Heinrich Hoffmann / CC-BY-SA 3.0. Accessible here: https://commons.wikimedia.org/wiki/File:Bundesarchiv_Bild_146-1987-004-09A,_Amin_al_Husseini_und_Adolf_Hitler.jpg

Source 14: Public Domain. Schmidt, Dana Adams. "AIM TO OUST JEWS PLEDGED BY SHEIKH", New York Times. August 2, 1948. Publicly available preview of the article, accessible here: https://Acknowledgements .nytimes.com/1948/08/02/archives/aim-to-oust-jews-pledged-by-sheikh-head-of-moslem-brotherhood-says.html

Source 15: Extract from Flapan, Simha. "The Palestinian Exodus of 1948." Journal of Palestine Studies 16, no. 4 (1987): 3–26.

Source 16: Public domain. Albert Einstein Letter to The New York Times. December 4, 1948 New Palestine Party. Visit of Menachen Begin and Aims of Political Movement Discussed. Accessible here: https://archive.org/details/AlbertEinsteinLetterToTheNewYorkTimes.December41948

Source 17: Public domain. Congress.gov. "Congressional Record." December 1, 1947 Vol. 93, Part 9 — Bound Edition. 80th Congress - 1st Session - Senate pages 10984. Accessible here: https://Acknowledgements .congress.gov/bound-congressional-record/1947/12/01/93/senate-section/article/10949-10991

Source 18: Public domain. United Nations Partition Plan

Source 19: Public Domain. "200 DISPLACED ARABS RETURN TO THEIR VILLAGE UNDER UN AUSPICES", Press Release PAL/537, 4 November 1949. UNITED NATIONS, Department of Public Information (DPI), Press and Publications Bureau, Lake Success, New York. Accessible here: https://Acknowledgements .un.org/unispal/document/auto-insert-208243/

Source 20: Public Domain. Unknown author / hanini.org / PD Syria / Wikimedia. Accessible here: https://commons.wikimedia.org/wiki/File:Man_see_school_nakba.jpg

CHAPTER 5

Chapter photo: Public domain. / IDF Spokesperson's Unit / Wikimedia / CC BY-SA 3.0. Accessible here: https://commons.wikimedia.org/wiki/File:Six-Day_War._IDF_14th_Armored_Brigade.jpg

Source 1: Extract to the preamble to the decisions taken at the Arab League Summit in Cairo, 1964. As cited in: Shlaim Avi. 2001. The Iron Wall : Israel and the Arab World. London: Penguin, pp. 229-230

Source 2: Public Domain. Extract from Letter dated 27 July 1968 from the Permanent Representative of Israel to the United Nations addressed to the Secretary General. Accessible here: https://digitallibrary.un.org/record/517014/files/S_8654-EN.pdf

Source 3: Public domain. Irgun / Wikimedia. Accessible here: https://commons.wikimedia.org/wiki/File:Irgun_poster_Erez_Jisrael.jpg

Source 4: "The East Bank of the Jordan" Ze'ev Jabotinsky, 1929. Accessible here: https://web.archive.org/web/20070928015519/http://Acknowledgements .zfa.org.il/articles/jabotinsky.html

Source 5: YLittle Savage / Wikimedia Commons/ CC BY-SA 3.0 Accessible here: https://commons.wikimedia.org/wiki/File:Black_Arrow_Memorial_07.jpg

Source 6: Public domain. Moshe Pridan / Wikimedia / National Photo Collection of Israel, Photography dept. Government Press Office, under the digital ID D275-041 (http://gpophotoeng.gov.il/fotoweb/Grid.fwx?search=D275-041.jpg#Preview1). Image accessible here: https://commons.wikimedia.org/wiki/File:Fedayeen_1956.jpg

Source 7: Extract from Lenczowski, George. "Arab Bloc Realignments." Current History 53, no. 316 (1967): 346–84. http://Acknowledgements .jstor.org/stable/45311809

Source 8: Public domain. Unknown author / Wikimedia. Accessible here: https://commons.wikimedia.org/wiki/File:Samu_Incident.jpg

Source 9: Extract from Morris Benny. 2001. Righteous Victims : A History of the Zionist-Arab Conflict 1881-1999. New York: Knopf, pp. 303-4

Source 10: Public domain. Extract from the 1949 Israeli-Syrian General Armistice Agreement. Accessible here: https://digitallibrary.un.org/record/471866?ln=zh_CN

Source 11: Public domain. Address by Prime Minister Begin at the National Defense College- 8 August 1982. Accessible here: http://web.archive.org/web/20160208060552/http://Acknowledgements .mfa.gov.il/mfa/foreignpolicy/mfadocuments/yearbook6/pages/55%20address%20by%20prime%20minister%20begin%20at%20the%20national.aspx

Source 12: Extract from Shlaim Avi. 2001. The Iron Wall : Israel and the Arab World. London: Penguin, pp. 237

Source 13: Graph courtesy of tradingeconomics.com, based on World Bank data. Data and graph accessible here: https://tradingeconomics.com/israel/gdp

Source 14: Extract from Sarah Ozacky-Lazar. "'The Seven Good Years?' Israel, 1967–1973: The Critical Change." Israel Studies 23, no. 3 (2018): pp. 18. http://Acknowledgements .jstor.org/stable/10.2979/israelstudies.23.3.04

Source 15: Dr. Avishai Teicher via the PikiWiki - Israel Free Image Collection Project (http://Acknowledgements .pikiwiki.org.il?action=gallery&img_id=8321) / Wikipedia / CC BY 2.5. Accessible here: https://en.wikipedia.org/wiki/File:PikiWiki_Israel_8321_shalom_meir_towertel-aviv.jpg

Source 16: Plotzker, Sever, 'Economic' supplement for Independence Day, "Yediot Achronot" newspaper, 23 April 2007, and p. 2-3. "Israeli Economic History: Israel's Economy From 1967 Six Day War until 2007 - From Socialism to Capitalism I Historama.com The Online History Shop." Israeli Militaria, Coins, Israeli Stamps, Banknotes, Ephemera, Judaica & Israeli Music, History, Bauhaus Architecture & Online Collectibles Auctions. http://Acknowledgements .historama.com/online-resources/articles/israel/israeli_economy_since_six_day_war_1967_2007.html

Source 17: Extract from Shlaim Avi. 2001. The Iron Wall : Israel and the Arab World. London: Penguin, pp. 237

Source 18: Public domain. Ashashyou / Al Farida / Wikimedia. Accessible here: https://commons. wikimedia.org/wiki/File:Egypt_propaganga_1967_10.jpg

Source 19: Uri Bar-Noi, "The Soviet Union and the Six-Day War: Revelations From the Polish Archives," Cold War International History Project (CWIHP) e-Dossier No.8. Accessible here: https:// Acknowledgements .wilsoncenter.org/publication/the-soviet-union-and-the-six-day-war-revelations-the-polish-archives

Source 20: Public domain. Foreign Relations of the United States, 1964–1968, Volume XIX, Arab-Israeli Crisis and War, 1967, eds. Harriet Dashiell Schwar and Edward C. Keefer (Washington: Government Printing Office, 2004), Document 124. Accessible here: https://history.state.gov/ historicaldocuments/frus1964-68v19/d124

CHAPTER 6

Chapter photo: Efi Sharir / Photographer: Israel Press and Photo Agency (I.P.P.A.) / Dan Hadani collection, National Library of Israel / CC BY 4.0. Accessible here: https://commons.wikimedia.org/ wiki/File:Intifada_in_Gaza_Strip,_1987_II_Dan_Hadani_Archive.jpg

Source 1: Extract from Gail Pressberg (1988) 'The Uprising: Causes and Consequences', Journal of Palestine Studies, 17:3, 38-50

Source 2: Abarrategi / Wikimedia / CC BY-SA 4.0. Accessible here: https://commons.wikimedia.org/ wiki/File:Arton8011.jpg

Source 3: Map produced by Palestinian Academic Society for the Study of International Affairs (PASSIA). Accessible here: Acknowledgements .passia.org/maps/view/15

Source 4: Public domain. Unknown author / Wikimedia. Accessible here: https://commons. wikimedia.org/wiki/File:Swedish_peacekeepers_evacuating_their_position_during_the_Six_Day_ War.jpg

Source 5: Public domain. Accessible here: https://irp.fas.org/world/para/docs/880818a.htm

Source 6: Extract from Brandenburg, R., 2010. Iran and the Palestinians. The Iran Primer: Power, Politics, and US Policy, pp.171-174. Accessible here: http://iranprimer.usip.org/sites/default/files/Iran%20Region_Brandenburg_Palestinians%20Jan%202016.pdf

Source 7: Efi Sharir, Israel Press and Photo Agency (I.P.P.A.) / Dan Hadani collection, National Library of Israel /

CC BY 4.0. This image is available from National Library of Israel under the digital ID. (https://Acknowledgements .nli.org.il/en/archives/NNL_ARCHIVE_AL004027158/NLI) (990040271580205171). Accessible here: https://commons.wikimedia.org/wiki/File:Intifada_in_Gaza_Strip,_1987_I_Dan_Hadani_Archive.jpg

Source 8: / Wikimedia / CC BY-SA 3.0. Accessible here: https://commons.wikimedia.org/wiki/File:Intifada_erase_slogan.jpg

Source 9: No known copyright restrictions. Warren K. Leffler / Wikipedia. This image is available from the United States Library of Congress's Prints and Photographs division under the digital ID ppmsca.03424. Accessible here: https://en.m.wikipedia.org/wiki/File:Sadat_Carter_Begin_handshake_(cropped)_-_USNWR.jpg

Source 10: Extract from McDowall David. 1989. 'Palestine and Israel : The Uprising and Beyond'. London: Tauris.

Source 11: Public domain. Accessible here: https://andyreiter.com/wp-content/uploads/military-justice/il/Laws%20and%20Decrees/Israel%20-%201967%20-%20Order%20No.%20101%20Regarding%20the%20Prohibition%20of%20Acts%20of%20Incitement%20and%20Hostile%20Propaganda.pdf

Source 12: Public domain.

Source 13: Public domain, Statistical abstracts of Israel, 1970-1980, Central Bureau of Statistics.

Source 14: Extract from the Jewish Virtual Library. Accessible here: https://Acknowledgements .jewishvirtuallibrary.org/myths-and-facts-the-palestinian-uprisings

Source 15: Yitzhak Rabin, extract in the Jerusalem Post 15 Feburary 1985, quoted in Sayigh, Institute for Palestine Studies (Washington D.C.). 2011. 'Armed Struggle and the Search for State : The Palestinian National Movement 1949-1993'. Oxford: Oxford University Press, pp. 608

Source 16: Extract from Diwan Ishac Radwan S Shaban and Palestine Economic Policy Research Institute (MAS) and the World Bank. 1999. 'Development Under Adversity : The Palestinian Economy in Transition'. Washington D.C: World Bank.

Source 17: Extract from Be'er Yizhar 'Abd al-Jawād Şāliḥ and Be-tselem (Organization : Jerusalem). 1994. 'Collaborators in the Occupied Territories : Human Rights Abuses and Violations'. Jerusalem: B'tselem

Source 18: Extract from Morris Benny. 2001. 'Righteous Victims : A History of the Zionist-Arab Conflict 1881-2001' First Vintage books edition ed. New York: Vintage Books.

Source 19: Figures compiled by B'TSelem The Israeli Information Center for Human Rights in the Occupied Territories. Accessible here: https://Acknowledgements .btselem.org/statistics/first_intifada_tables

Source 20: Public Domain. UNSCR Resolution 607. Accessible here: http://unscr.com/en/resolutions/doc/607

CHAPTER 7

Chapter photo: Public Domain, Photograph of the White House Photograph Office (Clinton Administration), Accessible here: https://catalog.archives.gov/id/183374092

Source 1: Wikimedia Commons by deutch_laender. Accessible here: https://commons.wikimedia.org/wiki/File:Sabra_Shatila_in_2003.jpg

Source 2: Fair Use extract from Denis Ross opinion piece in the NYT. Accessible here: https://www.nytimes.com/2023/10/12/opinion/israel-palestinians-gaza-peace.html

Source 3: Wikipedia Commons data taken from UN's OCHA Accessible here: https://en.wikipedia.org/wiki/Israeli_occupation_of_the_West_Bank#/media/File:Settlements2006.jpg

Source 4: Fair Use extract from Reuters' report of UN High Commissioner's statement. Accessible here: https://www.reuters.com/world/middle-east/israeli-settlements-expand-by-record-amount-un-rights-chief-says-2024-03-08/

Source 5: Fair Use extract from article in the Washington Institute for Near East Policy by Ghaith al-Omari Accessible here: https://www.reuters.com/world/middle-east/israeli-settlements-expand-by-record-amount-un-rights-chief-says-2024-03-08/

Source 6: Creative Commons 4.0 international License Accessible here: https://commons.wikimedia.org/wiki/File:Rocket_Attacks_fired_at_Israel_from_the_Gaza_Strip_by_year.png

Source 7: Fair use extract, Edward Said, 'The Morning After', London Review of Books, Vol. 15 No.20 Accessible here: https://www.lrb.co.uk/the-paper/v15/n20/edward-said/the-morning-after

Source 8: Fair Use. Extract from report on statement by Merav Michaeli. Accessible here: https://www.timesofisrael.com/labor-chief-michaeli-rabin-was-assassinated-with-netanyahus-cooperation/

Source 9: Public Domain. From the Ali Khamenei website. Accessible here: https://commons.wikimedia.org/wiki/File:Hamas_leader_Ismail_Haniyeh_meeting_Iranian_Supreme_Leader_Ali_Khamenei.jpg

Source 10: Creative Commons. From the website of the President of the Russian Federation Accessible here: https://commons.wikimedia.org/wiki/File:Vladimir_Putin_with_Yasser_Arafat-2.jpg

Source 11: Public information from OCHA (the United Nations Office for the Coordination of Humanitarian Affairs) Accessible here: https://www.ochaopt.org/content/humanitarian-snapshot-casualties-context-demonstrations-and-hostilities-gaza-30-march-12-0

Source 12: Public Domain. UNRWA website. Accessible here: https://www.unrwa.org/what-we-do/education

Source 13: Wikimedia Commons. Government press Office Israel. Accessible here: https://commons.wikimedia.org/wiki/File:Flickr_-_Government_Press_Office_(GPO)_-_King_Hussein_of_Jordan_lights_P.M.Yitzhak_Rabin%27s_cigarette_at_royal_residence_in_Akaba.jpg

Source 14: Public Domain. Wikicommons. Accessible here: https://commons.wikimedia.org/wiki/File:President_Trump_and_The_First_Lady_Participate_in_an_Abraham_Accords_Signing_Ceremony_(50345629858).jpg

Source 15: Fair use. Extract from article in The National News by Hugh Naylor Accessible here: https://www.thenationalnews.com/uae/russian-immigrants-have-pushed-israel-to-the-right-1.393835/

Source 16: Fair Use. Extract from article in Sky News online by Adam Boulton. Accessible here: https://news.sky.com/story/netanyahus-majoritarian-power-grab-is-tearing-society-apart-and-delighting-israels-enemies-12929102

Source 17: Public Domain Google Art project. Accessible here: https://en.wikipedia.org/wiki/Medieval_antisemitism#/media/File:Master_of_Vallbona_de_les_Monges_(Guillem_Seguer_?)_-_Altarpiece_of_the_Corpus_Christi_-_Google_Art_Project_(cropped).jpg

Source 18: Licensed under Creative Commons photographer Gideon Markowitz. Accessible here: https://en.m.wikipedia.org/wiki/File:Ramat_Gan_bus_bombing._Dan_Hadani_Archive_I.jpg

Source 19: Creative Commons Author Harry Pockets. Accessible here: https://commons.wikimedia.org/wiki/File:Huwwara_Checkpoint_Palestine.jpg

Source 20: Wikimedia Commons. Data from United Nations specifically OCHAoPT. Accessible here: https://commons.wikimedia.org/wiki/File:Timeline_of_Israel-Palestine_fatalities_2008-2023.png

CHAPTER 8

Source 1: Public Domain, Al-Fatah, "Press Release number 1", Beirut, 1 January 1968, Accessible here: https://www.palquest.org/en/historictext/33974/fatah-palestine-national-liberation-movement-press-release

Source 2: Y. Sayigh, Armed State and the Struggle for State: The Palestinian National Movement, 1949-1993, (Oxford University Press, 2004), p.162

Source 3: Public Domain, Article 12 of the Hamas Covenant of 1988, Accessible here: https://avalon.law.yale.edu/20th_century/hamas.asp

Source 4: Quote from I.Black, 'Hamas founder Sheikh Yassin interviewed', The Guardian, 8 September 1988, Accessible here: https://www.theguardian.com/world/2023/oct/10/from-the-archive-1988-hamas-founder-sheikh-yassin-interviewed

Source 5: Quote from, P.Hofmann, 'Dramatic Session', New York Times, 14 November 1974, Accessible here: https://www.nytimes.com/1974/11/14/archives/dramatic-session-plo-head-says-he-bears-olive-branch-and-guerrilla.html

Source 6: Public Domain, Accessible here: https://commons.wikimedia.org/wiki/File:Nasser_brokering_ceasefire_with_Chairman_Arafat_and_King_Hussein.jpg

Source 7: Public Domain, Oslo Accords Map, Accessible here: https://commons.wikimedia.org/wiki/File:Oslo_Areas_and_barrier_projection_2005.png

Source 8: Quoted in T.Baconi, Hamas Contained: The Rise and Pacification of Palestinian Resistance, (Stanford University Press, 2018), p.45

Source 9: Public Domain, the Palestinian Declaration of Independence, Accessible here: https://en.wikisource.org/wiki/Palestinian_Declaration_of_Independence

Source 10: Public Domain, Accessible here: https://commons.wikimedia.org/wiki/File:Bill_Clinton,_Yitzhak_Rabin,_Yasser_Arafat_at_the_White_House_1993-09-13.jpg

Source 11: Quoted in K.Hroub, 'A "New Hamas" through Its New Documents', Journal of Palestine Studies, Vol. 35. No. 4 (Summer 2006), pp.8-9

Source 12: Public Domain, Map showing Palestine election results 2006, Accessible here: https://commons.wikimedia.org/wiki/File:Palestine_election_results_2006.svg

Source 13: Photo of Abu Dis Wall, licensed under Creative Commons, Accessible here: https://commons.wikimedia.org/wiki/File:AbuDisWall.jpg

Source 14: Quote by Shlomo Ben Ami on Democracy Now!, 14 February 2006, Transcript. Accessible here: https://www.democracynow.org/2006/2/14/fmr_israeli_foreign_minister_shlomo_ben

Source 15: Own graph, Data from United Nations Office for the Coordination of Humanitarian Afairs, Accessible here: https://www.ochaopt.org/data/casualties

Source 16: Public Domain, Article 13 of the Hamas Covenant of 1988 (see Source 3); Article 20 of the Hamas Charter of 2017, Accessible here: https://www.wilsoncenter.org/article/doctrine-hamas

Source 17: Public Domain, International Monetary Fund Country Report No. 2023/327, 'West Bank and Gaza: Selected Issues', 13 September 2023, Accessible here: https://www.imf.org/en/Publications/CR/Issues/2023/09/12/West-Bank-and-Gaza-Selected-Issues-539154

Source 18: Public Domain, Public Opinion Polls by the Palestinian Center for Policy and Survey Research, Numbers 71-79, Accesible here: https://www.pcpsr.org/en/node/154

Source 19: Public Domain, 'Gaza Strip: The Humanitarian Impact of 15 years of the blockade', June 2022, United Nations Office for the Coordination of Humanitarian Affairs occupied Palestinian territory, Accessible here: https://www.unicef.org/mena/media/18041/file/Factsheet_Gaza_Blockade_2022.pdf.pdf

Source 20: Public Domain, Public Opinion Polls by the Palestinian Center for Policy and Survey Research, Numbers 87-91, Accesible here: https://www.pcpsr.org/en/node/154

CHAPTER 9

Chapter Photo: Creative Commons, Israel Defense Forces, Operation Protective Edge, Accessible here: https://www.flickr.com/photos/idfonline/14425209340"

Source 1: Public Domain. Protesters block Ayalon Highway demonstrating against Netanyahu's plans to suppress the Supreme Court Accessible here: https://commons.wikimedia.org/wiki/File:Demonstrating_against_judicial_reform_090323_17.jpg

Source 2: Public Domain. Photo credit: David Azagury, U.S. Embassy Jerusalem Wikimedia commons. Accessible here: https://commons.wikimedia.org/wiki/File:AmericanIsraeli_delegation_visit_to_Morocco,_December_2020_4350P_(50749122821).jpg

Source 3: Public Domain. UNICEF report. Accessible here: https://www.unicef.org/mena/documents/gaza-strip-humanitarian-impact-15-years-blockade-june-2022

Source 4: Public Domain. Wikimedia Commons. Accessible here: https://commons.wikimedia.org/wiki/File:Burnt_Car_in_Huwara.jpg

Source 5: Public Domain. Wikimedia Commons Map of Israel-Hamas attack 7-8th Oct 2024 Accessible here: https://commons.wikimedia.org/wiki/File:October_2023_Gaza%E2%88%92Israel_conflict_(7%E2%80%93_8_October)-ar.svg

Source 6: Public Domain Kobi Gideon / Government Press Office of Israel. Accessible here: https://en.m.wikipedia.org/wiki/File:Gaza_envelope_after_coordinated_surprise_offensive_on_Israel,_October_2023_(KBG_GPO06).jpg

Source 7: Reuters August 13 2020 reporting by Stephen Farrell Aljazeera August 15 2020. Accessible here: https://www.aljazeera.com/news/2020/8/15/how-the-world-reacted-to-uae-israel-normalising-diplomatic-ties https://www.reuters.com/article/idUSKCN2592T5/

Source 8: Reuters March 11,2024 reporting by Suleiman Al-Khalidi. Accessible here: https://www.reuters.com/world/middle-east/jordan-says-israels-al-aqsa-mosque-restrictions-risk-explosion-2024-03-11/

Source 9: Public Domain. Nato Strategic Communications Centre of Excellence. Accessible here: https://stratcomcoe.org/cuploads/pfiles/hamas_human_shields.pdf

Source 10: Public Domain. Wikimedia Commons Oren Rozen. Accessible here: https://commons.wikimedia.org/wiki/File:Iron_Swords_141023_Kirya_Bring_The_Home_02.jpg

Source 11: Public Domain. Distributed by Hamas Press Office and now widely available online

Source 12: Public Domain. Public statement from Amnesty official. Accessible here: https://www.amnesty.org/en/latest/news/2023/11/israel-opt-horrifying-cases-of-torture-and-degrading-treatment-of-palestinian-detainees-amid-spike-in-arbitrary-arrests/

Source 13: Public Domain. Wikimedia OpenStreetMap. Accessible here: https://en.wikipedia.org/wiki/Israel%E2%80%93Hamas_war_protests_in_the_United_States

Source 14: Institute for National Security Studies at Tel Aviv University. Accessible here: https://www.inss.org.il/publication/evacuation/

Source 15: Public Domain. Photo from the IDF Spokesperson's Unit. Accessible here: https://commons.wikimedia.org/wiki/File:Sol-War_23-11-01_IDF_13-08.jpg

Source 16: Public Domain. Public statement from the British Red Cross. Accessible here: https://www.redcross.org.uk/stories/disasters-and-emergencies/world/whats-happening-in-gaza-humanitarian-crisis-grows

Source 17: Creative Commons, Our World in Data, data source: Economist Intelligence Unit. Accessible here: https://ourworldindata.org/grapher/democracy-index-eiu

Source 18: Public Domain. Wikimedia Commons. Accessible here: https://commons.wikimedia.org/wiki/File:Merneptah_Steli_(cropped).jpg

Source 19: Public Domain. Wikipedia Andrew Shiva Nov 2013. Accessible here: https://en.wikipedia.org/wiki/Al-Aqsa_Mosque#/media/File:Jerusalem-2013-Temple_Mount-Al-Aqsa_Mosque_(NE_exposure).jpg

Source 20: Public Domain. Wikipedia by Reina91 April 2013. Accessible here: https://en.wikipedia.org/wiki/Palestinian_key#/media/File:The_Key_We_will_return,_taken_in_Jericho.jpg

Any income from the sale of this book will go to support the work of Parallel Histories, an educational charity based in the UK but working around the world.